In the Meantime:
Sermons for this Time Between the Times

Chris Currie

Parson's Porch Books

www.parsonsporchbooks.com

In the Meantime: Sermons for this Time Between the Times
ISBN: Softcover 978-1-946478-80-1
Copyright © 2018 by Chris Currie

Photo Credit: Neil Johnson

All scripture passages and scripture references are from the New Revised Standard Version, 1989, National Council of Churches.

All rights reserved. No part of this book may be reproduced or transmitted in any form or by any means, electronic or mechanical, including photocopying, recording, or by any information storage and retrieval system, without permission in writing from the publisher.

In the Meantime:
Sermons for this Time Between the Times

Contents

Contents 3
Foreword 7
Introduction 11

Part I: Advent

Beginning Again 13
    Mark 1:4-11

Vertical and Horizontal 19
    Mark 9:2-10

Learning to Fly 24
    I Thessalonians 4:13-18

Holiday Greetings from Mark 29
    Mark 13:24-37

Once More into the Mess 35
    Luke 1:39-56

All the King's Men 41
    Genesis 9:8-21

From Seeds to Weeds 47
    Matthew 13:24-30

More Than a Feeling 53
    1 John 4:7-21

Part II: Meantime

Nothing but Prodigals 59
    Ephesians 2:1-10

Plying the Church's Trade 66
    Matthew 18:15-20

How am I doing? 72
    Romans 6:1-11

A Hot Mess 77
    Matthew 27:11-26

Meanwhile... 83
    I Thessalonians 5:1-18

Who's Counting? 88
    Matthew 18:21-35

Tragic Necessity 94
    Habakkuk 2:1-4; Romans 5:1-5

Even the Unclean Spirits... 100
    Mark 1:21-28

Part III: Second Advent

Un-Godlike 109
    I Corinthians 1:18-25

Outliers 114
    Mark 1:14-20

Now Thank We All Our God 120
    Matthew 21:33-46

Both And... 126
    Matthew 25:31-46

Known by the Company You Keep 130
    Matthew 21:23-32

Easy Jesus 135
    Matthew 5:38-48

Unlocked 140
    John 20:19-31

Non-Ending 146
    Mark 16:1-8

Foreword

In two days I've been exposed to two bad sermons. Trust me. I've heard lots of bad sermons, even preached some myself so I'm an experienced judge of inept homiletics. On Saturday I attended the funeral of a friend of longstanding. She was active in her church and was a vibrant, though not unquestioning, believer. The preacher at her funeral seemed unaware -- or unconcerned -- about my deceased friend's relationship with Christ or her commitment to God's work. He went on at length about my friend's personal charm, her cooking ability, and her intelligence.

"And best of all, she was a grandmother who truly loved her grandchildren." Wow, what a remarkable achievement. Take that all you unaffectionate grandmothers!

It was a terrible funeral sermon, not because it was poorly delivered or badly constructed, but because it lacked theological interest or substance. The sermon implied that our hope in life, in death, in any life beyond death is in our charm, good cooking, and affectionate grandparenting. Jesus Christ failed to win even a cameo role in the sermon and everybody left the service with the impression that the Christian faith is silent and stupefied in the face of death.

The next day, in Duke Chapel, another unchristian sermon from a different preacher, different subject and setting, but bad in the same way as the sermon at the funeral. Lacking any interest in the assigned scripture, the preacher decided to attack the Trump administration (that takes guts when you're in the pulpit at Duke!). He listed various conventional attitudes slightly to the left of the Democratic Party and commended this as "incarnating our faith." Once again, Jesus Christ, or for that matter any member of the Trinity, managed to make only an insignificant appearance. Save yourself by yourself.

In my despair I received a salubrious gift from God – Chris Currie's book of sermons. *In the Meantime* is a demonstration of the fruitfulness of having a preacher who is thoroughly tethered to scripture and to a living, revealing God. Chris, unlike the preachers I heard the weekend before, agrees with his mentor, Karl Barth that the main test for a sermon is theological, Christological – how well does the preacher allow Christ to be with his people through the medium of preaching? As Barth said, the Bible is so much more interesting than the preacher, or us.

Because I got to see Chris in action in his lively congregation during a long, icy weekend (I'm referring to the frigid weather, not to his church's denomination label) I was unsurprised by the theological virtuosity of these sermons. Each is an invitation to the congregation to join in the joyful task of taking God more seriously and ourselves a little less so. Chris loves his congregation as much as the next preacher, but even more Chris loves the peculiar way Christ loves his people. Though these sermons are recognizably contextual, delivered at a specific time and place, the words of a contemporary pastor trying to get through to his congregation, Chris' sermons are always about God. That's no small achievement these days when what passes for preaching is mostly prattling about us.

In his sermons, on his way to talking about God, Chris moves easily from talk about Tom Petty to Karl Barth (his favorite theologian), from Willie Nelson to John Calvin (his next most beloved theologian). Though Chris admits that we are in a "hot mess," he is always able to see humor in our human condition. Chris somehow manages to avoid both sentimentality and moralizing advice, two of the curses of too much contemporary mainline preaching. In reading these sermons, you will have moments when you will marvel at how skillfully, how effortlessly and unpretentiously but interestingly Chris ladles out lively Reformed theology to his people. Though we know we are listening to an actual pastor who is deeply concerned that his congregation hear and receive his words, Scripture is Chris' primary interlocutor.

Every sermon in this collection is interesting and clear. The congregation knows it's in the hands of a competent communicator of the faith who begins a sermon knowing where he is headed. Each sermon clearly arises from the text, reaches out to everyday contemporary life, and then heads back to the text by the end, allowing the text to discipline the sermon's movement.

Chris' preaching reminds me of the theological dexterity of Fleming Rutledge, whose theologically based preaching Chris greatly admires. That's paying Chris a high compliment. Like Rutledge, Chris is convinced that the gospel is true and that while a sermon puts gospel truth in conversation with other truth claimants, the gospel is never subservient or servile to other truth competitors.

One day we shall clearly see ourselves with God without confusion or obfuscation. We shall allow ourselves to be loved by the God who, in Jesus Christ, has loved us. We shall know as we have been known and God will be all in all. In the meantime, read Chris Currie's sermons and take heart.

Will Willimon
Professor of the Practice of Ministry, Duke Divinity School, and United Methodist Bishop, retired, author of *How Odd of God: Chosen for the Curious Vocation of Preaching.*

Introduction

These sermons were preached over the span of a year sometime between 2017 and 2018 at First Presbyterian Church, Shreveport. Recently I had the opportunity to be present at Eugene Peterson's final public address at the Karl Barth Pastor's Conference on the campus of Princeton Theological Seminary. Because of Eugene Peterson's declining health, the address ended up being read by his son Eric. The whole address and talk were very moving and special. It was a privilege to be present and to be shaped once again by the words and writing of Eugene Peterson. In his address, which was an appreciation for the theology of Karl Barth, Peterson, in conversation with Barth, discussed the difficulties of sermons in written or book form. Perhaps a book is not the sermon's natural habitat. Sermons are events, occurrences, and attempts to declare the gospel of Jesus Christ to a particular people in a particular place in a particular time with particular concerns and particular events happening in their lives and in the life of the world. To write sermons down, to publish them, and to put them in book form risks removing them from the intimacy of the congregation in which they were preached, risks ripping them from the struggles a community may be facing, and risks placing them out of the intricacies of a congregation's context, setting, and ethos. All of this is true, and yet Peterson reminds us that there is still value in reading a sermon secondhand or putting the preached Word in published form, and that a 'prayerful imagination can and does supply much' of what might be lost when transported into a book. We Presbyterians are people of the Word and people of the word. We are people who are shaped and formed by the preaching and hearing of the gospel, but we are also people of the written word, people formed and shaped by the witness of scripture and the beauty of written language. As such, we place a high value on the use of words that express the Christian faith in ways that lead us to think and act and live beyond the presenting possibilities. So while these sermons and their words may be one step removed from the event of the gospel and the context in which they were proclaimed,

I trust they are of some value to the reader's life of faith. By engaging them with a prayerful imagination, I hope these sermons can offer a window into the ways I believe Christ is at work through the pages of scripture, through the voice of the preacher, and through the ministry of the congregation, moving beyond us and moving us beyond, into the life of our world, where we are called to be Christ's church 'out there.'

I want to thank the congregation that I serve, First Presbyterian Church, Shreveport, for the ways they make me want to be a better preacher, person, and disciple of Jesus Christ. I am grateful to serve with gifted colleagues on our ministry staff, support staff, and alongside congregation members and friends in ministry. I am grateful to be married to someone who takes the faith seriously, who seeks to live it out in our life together, and in our family. She is a delightful companion on this journey and we are nearly always surrounded by curious, funny, and loving children each and every day. I thank my parents for showing me so well what ministry could be and for taking the time to offer suggestions and corrections to what is before you. Special thanks to David Tullock and Parson's Porch Books for seeing something in these sermons worth putting into published form. And I thank all the congregations in which I have heard faithful and gifted preaching and in which I have seen congregations committed to the hearing of the Word as it becomes actualized in creative and vital forms of ministry. To these faithful and loving congregations, small and large, across town, city, and globe, Brenham Presbyterian Church, First Presbyterian Church Kerrville, Covenant Presbyterian Church Charlotte, Calypso Presbyterian Church, the Greyfriars Kirk congregation in Edinburgh, Scotland, and First Presbyterian Church, Shreveport, Louisiana, to all these congregations, I dedicate this book.

Part I: Advent

Beginning Again
Mark 1:4-11

John the baptizer appeared in the wilderness, proclaiming a baptism of repentance for the forgiveness of sins. And people from the whole Judean countryside and all the people of Jerusalem were going out to him, and were baptized by him in the river Jordan, confessing their sins. Now John was clothed with camel's hair, with a leather belt around his waist, and he ate locusts and wild honey. He proclaimed, "The one who is more powerful than I is coming after me; I am not worthy to stoop down and untie the thong of his sandals. I have baptized you with water; but he will baptize you with the Holy Spirit." In those days Jesus came from Nazareth of Galilee and was baptized by John in the Jordan. And just as he was coming up out of the water, he saw the heavens torn apart and the Spirit descending like a dove on him. And a voice came from heaven, "You are my Son, the Beloved; with you I am well pleased."

I hope I am not the only person who experiences this from time to time or I am going to feel self-conscious or embarrassed, but I always get a bit melancholy at the end of the year when a television show of some kind or other will do a tribute to stars and celebrities who have died in the past year. Maybe it reminds me of my mortality or of whatever ancillary role that specific actor or figure played at some point in my life, but when I see those tributes, I always get a sense of nostalgia but also melancholy. And it's not just television tributes that achieve such purposes, but as a Christian community when we recognize those who have died in the past year and remember them on the Sunday after All Saints Sunday, I carry with me similar emotions as I am sure we all do from time to time. One of those celebrity deaths that led me to do something slightly erratic and go on Amazon and order some of their CD's (which by the way I am told is an antiquated thing to do in this day and age), was the death of Tom Petty, who contributed a lot to the soundtrack of my youth and movement into young adulthood. So as we say goodbye to 2017 and Tom Petty and enter into a new year and new opportunities for discipleship together, as we turn the page on what is past, the title from one of Tom Petty's songs called 'Time to Move On,' reminds us that the proper posture of a Christian is to always look ahead.

Sometimes I have been accused by unnamed members of our household of liking songs and the tunes of songs without paying attention to the lyrics and then when paying attention to the lyrics having to rethink my affection for the song in question, but in this case, both the song and the lyrics have resonated with me and I think in a way are a good interpretation of what is going on in this passage and Mark's introduction and initiation of us and his audience into the life and ministry of Jesus. There is no stable or Mary and Joseph or angels, shepherds or wisemen. No star or Christmas carols or silent night. Just John the Baptist out in the wilderness proclaiming a baptism of repentance and Jesus beginning his life and his ministry by joining the crowds and seeking to be baptized by John.

In his post-Christmas poem 'So that is that,' W.H. Auden describes our Griswoldian failure to make this Christmas fulfill all our expectations: lukewarm leftovers, back to school, putting up all the decorations, and failing once again spectacularly to love our family—this is the imprint Christmas leaves behind.[1] Maybe if it doesn't happen for Christmas, then this will be the new year that

---

[1] W.H. Auden, 'So that is that,' in *The Oxford Book of Christmas Poems*, 142.

we become a new person or maybe it will happen this Lent as we pick up some new spiritual disciplines and gain mastery over our lives. Please do not misunderstand me...I am not against a Griswold family Christmas or keeping new year's resolutions or newfound Lenten disciplines that await us, but there is a cyclical nature to our lives and a constant revisiting of our goals and our failures that begins and ends, that starts and stops. We always seem to be beginning again. And in a way, so does scripture. Each time we come to it again, it has something new to say to us and shape us no matter how many times we have encountered it before and how much we think we already now. We have to begin again.

Perhaps one of the most meaningful quotations that I cling to comes from (as you might imagine) Karl Barth who wrote in 1948 that 'One never is a Christian, one can only become one again and again; in the evening of each day somewhat ashamed about one's Christianity of the day just over and in the morning of each new day glad that one may dare to be one all over again, doing so with solace, with one's fellow (human beings), with hope, with everything. The Christian congregation is of one mind in that it consists of real beginners.'[2] Christmas is only a beginning of which there will be many more beginnings. Mark's gospel does not even mention the birth of Jesus. Nor any visit to Egypt or getting lost in the temple or learning the carpentry trade from his father. For Mark, he only needs John's brief introduction, and then the baptism of Jesus which begins what is new and what is urgent and what needs to be made known to us. For Mark, this moment is where Jesus life and ministry peak in relevancy and intensity. We begin at his baptism in the Jordan. We will begin again with his transfiguration and again with his journey to the cross, and again

---

[2] Karl Barth, quotation on the wall at the Center of Barth Studies, Princeton, NJ. 1948.

with Good Friday and Easter and again with his ascension and Pentecost and again as we await his return. There is no static state of Christianity---no place of stasis and status quo---but rather each day we begin again as we seek to become part of this story and become part of Christ's ministry in our here and now.

I leave you with one last image and that is courtesy of the art on the cover of the bulletin which comes from the St. John's Bible which we were privileged to have here last February at our church retreat. In some ways one might see the prominent figure of this image as the one in the foreground who is John the Baptist, but though he remains central and prominent in this picture, his work is done, and we will not see him or hear his voice much until next Advent. The baptism of Jesus has already taken place and John remains the voice in the wilderness going on to carry out his ministry of repentance. The figure of Jesus remains in the background as the spirit of God anoints him, not for a ministry of solitude and repentance only, but a ministry of solidarity with sinners that leads to their redemption. So in this new year, let us say goodbye to Christmas and let us bid farewell to John the Baptist. Their work is done for now, and we begin again. In the words of Tom Petty, 'it is time to move on, time to get going, what lies ahead we have no way of knowing,' but though we begin again, we trust, we hope, and we expect, that Jesus' baptism and Jesus' life will once again transform our own baptism and transform our own lives and be detected and reflected in us however faintly and momentarily, so that we may become Christian again and again and again.

Vertical and Horizontal
Mark 9:2-10

Six days later, Jesus took with him Peter and James and John, and led them up a high mountain apart, by themselves. And he was transfigured before them, and his clothes became dazzling white, such as no one on earth could bleach them. And there appeared to them Elijah with Moses, who were talking with Jesus. Then Peter said to Jesus, 'Rabbi, it is good for us to be here; let us make three dwellings, one for you, one for Moses, and one for Elijah.' He did not know what to say, for they were terrified. Then a cloud overshadowed them, and from the cloud there came a voice, 'This is my Son, the Beloved; listen to him!' Suddenly when they looked around, they saw no one with them anymore, but only Jesus. As they were coming down the mountain, he ordered them to tell no one about what they had seen, until after the Son of Man had risen from the dead. So they kept the matter to themselves, questioning what this rising from the dead could mean.

There is a scene in the original Muppet Movie, does anyone remember that film which is now nearly forty years old? It stars Kermit the frog who is on the run from Doc Hopper who wants to coerce Kermit the frog into being the spokesperson for his Frog Leg franchise and he falls into company with Fozzie Bear and Dr. Teeth and the Electric Mayhem who are an eccentric funk band who ply their trade in an old Presbyterian church. My favorite line from the movie is Kermit the frog and Fozzie Bear walking into this old white clapboard Presbyterian Church and opening the door to find this cast of characters rocking it out like the P-Funk All Stars. As they walk in, Fozzie turns to Kermit after seeing this loud and wild band, and says, 'They don't look like Presbyterians to me.' And indeed, they probably don't. I have always chafed at some of the nicknames or epithets used to describe Presbyterians from 'frozen chosen' to Presbyterians do all things 'decently and in order' to unbending, stiff, humorless, dour, serious killjoys. And let's admit it, some of those monikers might hit the mark from time to time. But, when done well, there is nothing about our worship or our lives or our ethical commitments that resemble any of those categories or descriptions. If the point of worship is only to produce some kind of peppy and cosmetically happy narcotic that reduces the Christian faith to a very small emotional category of cloying and sentimental musical selections and references to God in terms of a divine boyfriend or girlfriend, then the whole anatomy of the human life and soul has made worship just about some small sector and substrata of self-help.

I can remember my father talking about a memory as a very small child sitting next to his mother in worship, and seeing her weeping in the midst of worship, and asking her what was wrong, and her reply was that 'she was just so happy.' Happiness and fulfillment can find us in some mysterious and roundabout ways that don't always have to involve a snare drum or a fog machine or a certain kind of proscribed form of canned happiness. All that is to say, at the same time, worship should never feel so comfortable that we are completely at home and at ease and never shocked by what happens here. Essayist and writer, Annie Dillard, reminds us that the God who called Moses also said to him, "come no closer! Remove the sandals from your feet, for the place on which you are standing is holy ground (Exodus 3:5)." but instead she writes, we often walk into worship 'babbling about golf and groceries, mindless of place.' At this point, she reminds us, 'ushers should issue life preservers and signal flares; they should lash us to our pews.'³

I think something like that happens to Peter and James and John on the mountaintop with Jesus. They are good Presbyterians and in the midst of the mysterious and mystical, they get anxious and nervous and wonder what on earth they can do to keep themselves busy in the presence of the holy One of Israel. 'Lord, I'm not completely comfortable with what is happening here, I'm not completely comfortable with awe in your presence, so how why don't we get busy and make some memorials while otherworldly worship is happening around us and we are afraid your transcendent presence is going to swallow us up.' Mark explains the situation perfectly in verse 6: 'Peter did not know what (else) to say, for he was terrified.' Most of the time we do not think of worship as terrifying, but I hope there is a sense that when we walk into this place we get a sense that life and worship and the Christian life are not just about us. Theologian James Torrance reminds us that Jesus does not just represent us or stand in our place for us on the cross alone, but does so in our worship together as well, often doing and redeeming what we failed to do, offering up to God the worship and praise we failed to offer or offered only limply. Jesus prays with us and for us offering up to God our sorrows and struggles and inner conflicts. 'He comes to stand in for us,' Torrance reminds us, 'when in our failure and bewilderment we do not know how to pray as we ought,' but Christ 'by his Spirit helps us in our infirmities.'⁴ So yes Peter and James and John are uncomfortable and terrified in the radiant presence of Christ on the mountaintop

---

³ From Annie Dillard, *Teaching a Stone to Talk*, in Tom Long, *Beyond the Worship Wars*, viii.

⁴ James B. Torrance, *Worship, Community, and the Triune God of Grace*, 14.

and are eager to memorialize the event and move on back down the hill toward reality.

But the Christian faith and the activity of worship need to have both the vertical and the horizontal. Professor of worship and preaching, Ron Byars writes that 'where there is no mystery—where even the most profound spiritual claims seem within the grasp of the intellect—the product is a certain barrenness,' and where everything is vertical and mystery and everything is cast loose from reason and the challenges of everyday life, 'there is likely to be superstition.' Byars thinks it is curious and strange that we live in a time and in a society that on the one hand 'produces churches [hostile to] and stripped of traditional ceremony that borrows instead 'models of therapeutic speech and concert,' while on the other hand exists "a New Age movement with crystals, candles, and out of body experiences with no evidence of being constrained by reason.'[5] In contrast, in the presence of Jesus Christ, there is both vertical and horizontal. The awe and reverence and wonder in the presence of the divine, but also as we see at the end of our passage and beyond, there is the impulse and movement back down the mountain, into the horizontal, not remaining forever in the rarified air of the spiritual mountaintop, but going back into the world to love it, transform it, and spread the reflection of God's glory everywhere. It cannot remain bottled up on top of the mountain, but must be put into practice, put to use, and risked on the world at the bottom of the mountain. Vertical and horizontal.

John Burgess is a Presbyterian theologian who took a sabbatical year, and along with his family moved to St. Petersburg, Russia for a year to immerse themselves in the life of a Russian Orthodox

---

[5] Ron Byars, *Christian Worship*, 32.

parish. What Burgess found in those Orthodox communities of faith was a strong sense of the vertical, in worship and icons, that sought to point them to the 'transformed reality that lives in and around us all the time.' While Burgess found that Orthodoxy is oriented almost exclusively to the vertical, he worries that American Christianity 'has lost the sense of standing before a holy God,' and 'authentic veneration and reverence' has been replaced by emotional manipulation. Loyalty to the apostolic faith has been reduced, he worries, to marketing religious services and we live in a context in his view where 'individuals refuse to say a creed until they have determined whether they agree with all of it.'[6]

But as we see in this Transfiguration story, there is both a vertical and a horizontal, a holy reverence standing before the mystery of God but also an impulse not to wallow on the mountaintop forever, but to make our way down the mountain to put this faith into practice, to embrace the needs and challenges of the world, and to offer others the gift we have been given. All disciples need both…the vertical and the horizontal. So may the transfiguration of Christ and the mystery on the mountaintop touch our hearts, souls, and minds with the mystery of God, and may it also transfigure our lives in Christ's service, so that vertically and horizontally, we follow until Christ's kingdom comes.

---

[6] Ron Byars, Book Review, John Burgess, *Encounters with Orthodoxy*, in the *Presbyterian Outlook*, December 27, 2013.

Learning to Fly
I Thessalonians 4:13-18

Paul's correspondence to the Thessalonians is the earliest literature contained in the New Testament, written about 15-20 years after the events of Christ's death and resurrection. As with most of Paul's letters, he is addressing a problem or crisis in the congregation and in the case of the Thessalonians there is anxiety about Christ's imminent return. The expectation in the early Christian community was that when the communion words were spoken, just as we speak today, that Christ has died, Christ has risen, and Christ will come again, that coming again would occur in that community's lifetime. The problem was that some members of the community were dying before Christ's return, and Paul's letter is a pastoral care letter of assurance about the dead, but also a letter of encouragement and hope to the living of how to live in this time between Christ's resurrection and Christ's return, a time that still characterizes our own time, as we continue to say and pray, 'Christ has died, Christ has risen, and Christ will come again.' Listen for the word of God:

> *But we do not want you to be uninformed, brothers and sisters, about those who have died, so that you may not grieve as others do who have no hope. For since we believe that Jesus died and rose again, even so, through Jesus, God will bring with him those who have died. For this we declare to you by the word of the Lord, that we who are alive, who are left until the coming of the Lord, will by no means precede those who have died. For the Lord himself, with a cry of command, with the archangel's call and with the sound of God's trumpet, will descend from heaven, and the dead in Christ will rise first. Then we who are alive, who are left, will be caught up in the clouds together with them to meet the Lord in the air; and so*

In the Meantime

we will be with the Lord forever. Therefore encourage one another with these words.

I can remember hearing depression-era stories about money stuffed under mattresses and jars buried in the backyard, thinking how strange and fearful such practices were. Could life really get that desperate and anxiety-ridden and fearful? That was before 2008 when an entire investment bank, a bank founded in 1850, a bank that had survived the Civil War, the Great Depression, the Cold War, September 11th and many other national crises, dissolved and went bankrupt in a span of 24 hours, nearly leading to the implosion of the entire worldwide economy. Okay, so this is why burying money in mattresses and in the backyard can seem like the safest option...in 1998, I was in my second year in the teaching profession, teaching a classroom full of 16 and 17 year olds, when news reports came in about students Dillon Klebold and Eric Harris, who if alive today would be in their late 30s, but who chose instead to inflict their pain on innocent school classmates and teachers leading to an epidemic of such events in our world from Las Vegas to Mother Emmanuel AME church to Sutherland Springs to Sandy Hook. And it is still weird to watch movies that include air travel prior to September 2001 as it looks so odd to see people walking to the terminal gate to wait for friends and loved ones and meet them at their gate or see people go through security lines that were only a minor hindrance. Even as our technological breakthroughs and quality of life continue to make life more efficient and comfortable, a multitude of studies show that anxiety levels are at the highest they have been over the 80-year period of recording the statistics. No matter what solutions we come up with, why are we still anxious? In an age of unprecedented economic expansion and quality of life, contentment, security, an anxiety free life is not only elusive, but farther away than ever.

It is not any better if you open up scripture and read it because the people in there are anxious and fearful people too. Listen to the first verse of the 43rd chapter of Isaiah: 'do not fear, for I have redeemed you; I have called you by name, you are mine....do not fear.' Well that's Isaiah and that's the Old Testament and it was a primitive age and they had a lot to worry about and be anxious about. Once Jesus comes along...all the anxiety goes away. Hear these words from Matthew 6:25: 'Therefore I tell you, do not worry about your life, what you will eat or what you will drink or about your body, what you will wear...do not worry about tomorrow, for tomorrow will bring worries of its own. Today's trouble is enough for today' (Matthew 6:25, 34). Well that was before Jesus was crucified and died and fixed everything.... that's why people are still worried and scared and anxious. Once that happens everything is okay. Yet after the resurrection we could turn to the 20th chapter of John, and in the 19th verse find the disciples hiding inside a house with the doors locked where the risen Christ finds them in fear and trembling. And here in our passage from Paul's letter to the church in Thessalonica, just a few years after Christ's resurrection, all we can find is a Christian community full of anxiety, worried about the future, and fretting over those who have died before Christ's return, certain they will miss out on the coming of the Lord. Fear, anxiety, worry, all seem to be, not only part of the human condition, but a very present characteristic in the life of the Christian community. It is not something we are ever without and God is not a genie-in-a-bottle who waves a wand and removes anxiety from us. It is part of our humanity. And yet a life of anxiety and paralysis due to fear is not the life God intends for us either, rather God helps us to live faithfully and to live with courage in the midst of anxiety and fear and worry. Do not worry, Paul, tells his fellow Christians in Thessalonica, God will bring back those who have died and reunite you with them in Christ...they are not lost, but will be raised and united with Christ even before the living so that we may all be caught up together and be united with the Lord forever (I Thessalonians 4:13-17). 'Then we who are alive, who are left, will be caught up in the clouds together with them to meet the Lord in the air; and so we will be with the Lord forever.'

One of my favorite contributions of John Calvin to our communion liturgy is the phrase 'lift up your hearts.' In his Genesis commentary, Calvin compares Christ to a ladder from heaven, a ladder that 'connects heaven and earth,' reaching down 'from heaven to earth,' the way all of God's 'celestial blessings flow down to us, and through which we, in turn, ascend to God.'[7] With Christ, we ascend to the Father. In trying to make peace between Lutherans and Zwinglians over communion differences, Calvin described the event of communion not as Jesus coming down into the elements or changing places with the elements, but as the Spirit of Christ uniting us through the sharing of the elements and lifting us up to the right hand of God by the power of the Holy Spirit. Lift up your hearts, is a prayer to be lifted up to God. It is not just an attempt to slap a 'smiley-face' on life.

Richard Neuhaus poignantly reminds us of attempts to do just that through an invitation he once heard to pray to God with 'happy hearts,' and he imagined someone 'in the third row from the back responding, 'no, I'm sorry. My wife is dying of cancer. My heart is not happy but broken. I do not want to give thanks but to rage against the unfairness of it all.' We want the peace that passes all understanding, not a 'painted smile.'[8] Still, when we are invited to lift up our hearts, and we respond that we lift them to the Lord. 'Broken, doubting, tranquil, joyful, terror-ridden,' anxious,

---

[7] John Calvin, *Comm. Genesis* 28:12 (CO 23.391), in Julie Canlis, *Calvin's Ladder: A Spiritual Theology of Ascent and Ascension*, 91.

[8] Richard J. Neuhaus, *Freedom for Ministry*, 142.

worried— 'whatever, we lift them to the Lord.'[9] We do not ignore the troubles or anxieties of the moment nor do we pretend that they do not exist, and neither do we let them overwhelm, enslave, and consume us. Rather, like the Thessalonians before us, we lift up our hearts and look to Christ, who having descended to earth, prepares us to ascend where God is, so that we will be with the Lord forever. No matter the real challenges, fears, and worries of the moment, we do not slap a smiley-face and a painted smile on the anxieties and challenges that confront us, nor do we succumb to them or let them rule over us, but we lift our eyes to Christ, we lift up our hearts, and we live each day with hope, until Christ's kingdom comes, until we are with the Lord forever. Amen.

---

[9] Richard J. Neuhaus, *Freedom for Ministry*, 154.

Holiday Greetings from Mark
Mark 13:24-37

'But in those days, after that suffering,
the sun will be darkened,
and the moon will not give its light,
and the stars will be falling from heaven,
and the powers in the heavens will be shaken.
Then they will see "the Son of Man coming in clouds" with great power and glory. Then he will send out the angels, and gather his elect from the four winds, from the ends of the earth to the ends of heaven. From the fig tree learn its lesson: as soon as its branch becomes tender and puts forth its leaves, you know that summer is near. So also, when you see these things taking place, you know that he is near, at the very gates. Truly I tell you, this generation will not pass away until all these things have taken place. Heaven and earth will pass away, but my words will not pass away. But about that day or hour no one knows, neither the angels in heaven, nor the Son, but only the Father. Beware, keep alert; for you do not know when the time will come. It is like a man going on a journey, when he leaves home and puts his slaves in charge, each with his work, and commands the doorkeeper to be on the watch. Therefore, keep awake—for you do not know when the master of the house will come, in the evening, or at midnight, or at cockcrow, or at dawn, or else he may find you asleep when he comes suddenly. And what I say to you I say to all: Keep awake.'

At least a couple of advertisers, perhaps in order to induce a little more holiday adrenaline and anxiety into our lives, have already started saying it is time and they are available for you to 'get your last-minute Christmas gifts.' It's only December 3rd. Today is the first day of Advent and its already time to get it all over with. We are chasing stability harder than ever and if we can just get those 'last-minute' Christmas gifts before Advent starts we can enjoy life and avoid the mess and instability of the season. But there is nothing stable or docile about what confronts us in scripture today. The prophet Isaiah cries out to the Lord in desperation: 'O that you would tear open the heavens and come down, so that the mountains would quake at your presence—as when fire kindles brushwood and the fire causes water to boil.' And we cannot rely on Mark for our holiday greetings either as he invites us to contemplate the coming of Christ, not as some pleasant holiday postcard, but as a turbulent event in which 'the sun will be darkened, and the moon will not give its light, and the stars will be falling from heaven, and the powers in the heavens will be shaken, and the Son of Man come in clouds with great power and glory.' Spooky. Strange. Unstable. Disruptive. These are sentiments that 'merry Christmas,' 'happy holidays,' or any other greeting card slogans fail to capture. The coming of this Lord and Messiah is disruptive, it will not leave us at ease or completely comfortable, and the good tidings of great joy that come with this Lord who tears open the heavens and comes down, will also undo us and remake us and reorder our lives and help us to see the kingdom of God, not up there or into the future, but right here, right now, among us.

The coming Christ prepares us to see in a way that is a bit off-kilter, imbalanced, and out of proportion to our normal ways of seeing and living. Ernest Campbell, former pastor of the Riverside Church in New York City expresses it this way: 'if you have ever seen someone in need and rushed on by, intent on your own agenda—you've been with the Priest and the Levite. If you've ever reflected on the reality of evil and your own participation in it—you've been to the Upper Room. If you've ever agonized in prayer over a life or death situation—you've been to Gethsemane. If you've ever betrayed a trust, you've been with Judas. If you've ever been tortured in spirit and faulted for a wrong you did not do—you've been to Golgotha. If you've ever left a situation discouraged, dejected and then been surprised by joy—you've been on the Emmaus road. If you've ever been grasped by the universality of Jesus Christ and found that all your achievements, your status, your pride has melted away like the snow in the sun—you've been with Paul on the road to Damascus.'[10] The coming Christ unsettles us and ensures that none of those human emotions are unique to us nor are they unrelated phenomena in our lives. As Christ's life continues to disrupt, shape, and reorder order our own, the coming Christ sweeps us up in his way of life in this world. Rushing past someone in need to get our gifts before December 1st has an alternative in the narrative of Jesus Christ's life. A dark night of the soul is something with which Jesus Christ is well acquainted. As is betrayal, broken relationships, and a life of reducing each other to status and achievements or lack thereof. And yet the coming Christ refuses to let such penultimate realities have the last word or ultimately define us. Instead though we are unsettled and unstable and disrupted by this coming Messiah, he also gives us hope and refuses to let our lives finally be defined by failure or defeat or self-absorption or other creative contrivings to express our lives apart from him.

Just this past week, I read Les and Cindy Morgan's letter about their work with the Church in Southeast Asia as they prepared to return. They talked about the places ministry takes them along 'rough narrow roads to small villages, mud-walled, dirt floored homes and to the bedsides of some of the poorest people in the world.' Not only does their work lead them into the 'harsh realities

---

[10] Ernest Campbell, 'Christian Way of Seeing,' from Donald McKim, *The Church: Presbyterian Perspectives*, 46.

of people's sufferings,' Les reminds us, but in such work they and we also learn 'the hard-humbling reality' of how limited the church is 'in her ability to ease (all) those sufferings' and solve everyone's problems. So what are we to do? We could just try to seize all we can out of life and leave everyone else for themselves. We can live our lives as if Jesus Christ's life has no impact on us whatsoever and just walk through this world numb. We can lock our doors, batten down the hatches, and live like hermits. But as those touched by the life of the coming Christ, we can do none of those things. As Les reminds us, no matter the circumstances, no matter the sufferings or challenges of the moment, no matter whether or not we have all that we need to go forward or are limited in our ability to fix the world around us or to solve everyone's problems, 'the church perseveres in her mission journey with the Advent hope of the fulfillment of God's purposes in what he has called her to do.'[11]

Living as a community of faith grounded in such persistent Advent hope is an unstable endeavor. It will cause us to see the world in all its fierceness and in all its beauty and hopefulness. It will cause us to take risks that may cost us something of our dignity or status or place in the world. It will cause us to desire more for our lives than the simplistic greeting card sentimentalities that offer us platitudes and make us feel good for a few minutes. The coming of Christ demands more from us and also gives more to us even as he disrupts our lives. Christ's coming calls our lives into question, invades us more deeply than religious sentimentality, and offers us a way of life that does not look all that glamorous or successful or achievement oriented...just faithful and unwavering and persistent

---

[11] 'Mission's Advent Hope of Fulfillment,' from Les and Cindy Morgan, November 30, 2017.

and encouraging, no matter the suffering, the brokenness, or the achievements and conquests all around us.

Tim Suttle, a writer and church planter in Kansas City, in a recent article and blog wrote that one of the great enemies of the Christian community is religious sentimentality. The problem with sentimentality, Suttle reminds us, is that it leads us to think faith is about experiencing a religious sentiment but should not really disrupt our lives or 'make a difference in the way we live our lives.' 'The sentimental church,' he declares, 'will devote their entire Sunday service to Mothers' Day/Father's Day—or worse yet, Valentine's Day…not that we don't appreciate our parents and sweethearts, but yielding precious worship time to the celebration of greeting card companies signals a much deeper problem: we have lost track of the story of God.'[12] Thankfully Advent reminds us that the coming Christ does not lose track of us in the midst of our attempts to domesticate and stabilize him. Miraculously, he is able to disrupt our dreams of a perfect Christmas, whether it comes through a friend in crisis or a stranger in need randomly in our path or a way of life that challenges the despair and the shallow sentimentality of our world with a kingdom of God that embodies justice and peace and joy in the Holy Spirit.

In case you are interested in the process, no sermon comes together in exactly the same way. It's never an easy or flawless process and sometimes there is the need of external pressure of a deadline or an extra cup of coffee or an inner existential struggle to reach completion. And sometimes events outside our control happen and lead us down a different path. This past Friday was no exception. I received a phone call in the middle of my angst-ridden preparation time that a church member who has not been in good

---

[12] Tim Suttle, 'How to Shrink Your Church,' huffingtonpost.com/tim-suttle/, 1.

health for some time was leaving abruptly and moving away very soon and there was a small window of time to say goodbye and wish him well before he left to be closer to his family far away. There had been some family healing and reconciliation after a time of estrangement and now there was an opportunity for support and greater care, but it meant going away and leaving this community behind. In the hospital room, there was a weird mix of emotions, sadness in saying good bye, but happiness and joy in seeing reconciliation and a path forward rather than flailing and continued uncertainty. We said our goodbyes and had a prayer together and as I walked back out into the sunshine and traffic and a looming deadline, I also had a glisten in my eye and a feeling of thanksgiving. I am not 100% sure, but I think the coming Christ was trying to disrupt and dislodge me to remind me once again how significant and beautiful and wonderful the church is in all our comings and goings. A strange collection of people thrown together who embrace each other and support each other and reconcile with each other, a community, throughout all life's comings and all our goings, a community of imperfect people willing to be disrupted and displaced and put back together and made into something even greater than all the sum of our parts, through the work of the coming Christ.

Undone and put back together again. O come, O come Emmanuel.

Once More into the Mess
Luke 1:39-56

In those days Mary set out and went with haste to a Judean town in the hill country, where she entered the house of Zechariah and greeted Elizabeth. When Elizabeth heard Mary's greeting, the child leapt in her womb. And Elizabeth was filled with the Holy Spirit and exclaimed with a loud cry, 'Blessed are you among women, and blessed is the fruit of your womb. And why has this happened to me, that the mother of my Lord comes to me? For as soon as I heard the sound of your greeting, the child in my womb leapt for joy. And blessed is she who believed that there would be a fulfilment of what was spoken to her by the Lord.'

And Mary said,
'My soul magnifies the Lord,
  and my spirit rejoices in God my Saviour,
for he has looked with favour on the lowliness of his servant.
  Surely, from now on all generations will call me blessed;
for the Mighty One has done great things for me,
  and holy is his name.
His mercy is for those who fear him
  from generation to generation.
He has shown strength with his arm;
  he has scattered the proud in the thoughts of their hearts.
He has brought down the powerful from their thrones,
  and lifted up the lowly;
he has filled the hungry with good things,
  and sent the rich away empty.
He has helped his servant Israel,
  in remembrance of his mercy,

> *according to the promise he made to our ancestors,*
> *to Abraham and to his descendants forever.'*
>
> *And Mary remained with her for about three months and then returned to her home.*

There are emotions we have that words cannot always capture, and often with English it's the case where we just find that emotion better expressed in another language and adapt it for our own. One such case that comes to mind that is a particular challenging emotion is the German word *schadenfreude*. *Schaden* is the German word for 'bad' and *freude* is the German word for 'joy' which is a strange combination until you realize that the word is trying to depict that really sinful and nasty emotion we are all in danger of experiencing from time to time. Taking pleasure in the misfortune of others. *Schadenfreude*. Why would we ever feel that or admit to that…I think it is because we all have that base fight or flight instinct that thinks from time to time, 'I am glad I am not in his or her shoes, or I am glad that is not happening to me,' and the German language was able to put together a word that captures it perfectly. 'Bad joy.' *Schadenfreude*.

But here in this passage from Luke when Mary becomes a herald of good news and messenger of the gospel, '*schadenfreude*' is not an apt description of what is going on here, but a kind of a reverse '*schadenfreude*,' another emotion we do not really have a word for, when someone is joyful and really has no right to be. There is no word for it except that I think the emotion could be summed in a statement like 'what on earth reason do they have to be happy about?' Ever felt that one? I have. And it is what makes Mary's joy and her good tidings of great joy shine through in this passage.

In the Meantime

As we prepare once again for the unexpected...yes I am talking about the Christmas Pageant tonight...I was struck recently by an account of a Christmas pageant at a small town church in Minnesota in which Michael Lindvall described a revised script after 46 years of one formulaic pageant in that little church year after year. One of the changes in the script was a switch from the King James Version to the Good News translation of scripture and that changes had serious implications in the pageant. In the King James, the narrator described Mary's situation as being 'great with child,' but as the new regime updated the pageant, they rightly thought, 'what kid knows what 'great with child means?' 'The Good News translation (was) much more direct at this point. So, as Mary and Joseph entered, the Narrator read, 'Joseph went to register with Mary who was promised in marriage to him. She was pregnant.' Not great with child but pregnant. Lindvall recalls that 'as the last word echoed from the Narrator through the PA system into the full church, our little Joseph, hearing it, froze in his tracks, gave Mary an incredulous look, peered out at the congregation, and said, 'Pregnant? What do you mean pregnant?' This, of course, brought down the house. My wife, wiping tears from her eyes, leaned over to me and said, 'You know, that may well be just what Joseph actually said.'[13]

Nothing about this story, even the joyful parts like Mary's *Magnificat*, leave us feeling completely confident or comfortable. I mean is this the best God can really do? Place the whole divine enterprise in the life of a not yet married teenage peasant girl from the Jewish countryside? Is that really the plan? In a recent essay, I read a quotation from last year's Murray lecturer, David Fergusson

---

[13] Michael Lindvall, 'The Christmas Pageant, in *The Good News from North Haven*, 14-15.

who stated that 'the world was made so that Christ was born.'[14] Unpacking that a bit, Fergusson is reminding us that from the very beginning God's intention was to become human and walk in our shoes and enter into communion with us. This was not an emergency plan or a plan B when nothing else was working, but the very heart of who God is to never be God without us. Which makes it more astonishing that such a well hatched plan would unfold in such messy circumstances among such all-so-ordinary folk. Really? You are going to do this in this backwater town with a heretofore unheard of teenage peasant girl and her lukewarm bumbling surprised-looking husband? No well-established family...as we learn from Jesus' genealogy from Matthew, sure it includes Abraham and David, but it also includes some more suspect characters like Rahab and foreigner Ruth and a wild-eyed cousin in John the Baptist who we heard from last week. Couldn't God do better or make it easier? Couldn't God pick a less fragile and messy way to reconcile and redeem us?

I was thinking just such thoughts as I read this week an article about Facebook and social media in general that those early creators of social media platforms were now regretting some of their involvement as they realized some of their creations were now 'ripping apart the social fabric of our society,' by taking advantage of computer logarithms that create 'filter bubbles' and shield us from contrary beliefs and alternative views, choosing instead to share information that only confirms and contorts with what we already believe and denigrates what we are already inclined to

---

[14] David Fergusson, *Chapter 4: Creation*, 76-7 in *The Oxford Handbook of Systematic Theology*, edited by John Webster, Kathryn Tanner, and Iain Torrance.

disagree about.[15] Are you really willing to put it all in the line and put the salvation of the world all into the hands of this peasant girl? And can such a child really have it in himself to overcome a world stack against him and against us, with unseen logarithms tearing up our lives even as everything presents happy and fulfilled and airbrushed to perfection on the surface? And sometimes the messes in our life are not buried away in some Google algorithm trying to lead us where we think we want to be led but are more visible pressures…keeping up with Jones's or having no margin for error or time to sing like Mary sings.

Many years ago, when I was in seminary there was a cafeteria worker who worked the register and whenever we saw him we would ask him how he was doing, and he would always reply: 'I'm surviving.' But God did not make the world and enter into it just so we could survive and tread water. He came so that we might find our vocation, our purpose, our role we can play and contribution we can make so that we can do more than survive but rejoice and flourish in the life unfolding before us. Sometimes that life can feel overwhelming…it felt that way this week standing in two inches of water in my bathroom at the end of a long day only to find the dog had just eaten the sandwiches packed for the next day's lunch. It can feel that way in our world when our heroes turn out to be frauds and partisan politics makes us wish we were ostriches.

But one of the reasons Mary still sings the Lord's song is because she knows that God is not afraid of the mess, that God loves the mess of our world enough to enter into it, and that God can find no mess that is unredeemable. How on earth can she be happy? Doesn't she know what is ahead of her, all the heartache and

---

[15] Barbara Ortutay, 'Facebook's early friends now its sharpest critics,' *Shreveport Times*, Thursday, December 14, 2017, 10A.

heartbreak and what happens to the Messiah? How can she sing and rejoice and find her voice in such a mess? But Mary sings because she can sense the hand of God, even in the middle of the mess, and because she sees how she can be used to serve God's purposes, to find her role in the divine enterprise. So yes, the world is a mess...it was for Mary and it is for us. But that is not late breaking news nor is that the end of the story. The mess is not all that miraculous. What is miraculous is that Mary can rejoice and serve God's purposes in the middle of the mess and despite the mess.

Can we?

All the King's Men
Genesis 9:8-21

Then God said to Noah and to his sons with him, "As for me, I am establishing my covenant with you and your descendants after you, and with every living creature that is with you, the birds, the domestic animals, and every animal of the earth with you, as many as came out of the ark. I establish my covenant with you, that never again shall all flesh be cut off by the waters of a flood, and never again shall there be a flood to destroy the earth." God said, "This is the sign of the covenant that I make between me and you and every living creature that is with you, for all future generations: I have set my bow in the clouds, and it shall be a sign of the covenant between me and the earth. When I bring clouds over the earth and the bow is seen in the clouds, I will remember my covenant that is between me and you and every living creature of all flesh; and the waters shall never again become a flood to destroy all flesh. When the bow is in the clouds, I will see it and remember the everlasting covenant between God and every living creature of all flesh that is on the earth." God said to Noah, "This is the sign of the covenant that I have established between me and all flesh that is on the earth." The sons of Noah who went out of the ark were Shem, Ham, and Japheth. Ham was the father of Canaan. These three were the sons of Noah; and from these the whole earth was peopled. Noah, a man of the soil, was the first to plant a vineyard. He drank some of the wine and became drunk, and he lay uncovered in his tent.

It had been a pretty epic Lent for Noah. Here in Genesis 9 we encounter him just after the ark and as you can see in the bulletin art today, he builds an altar to the Lord and begins preparing burnt offerings on that altar. After the cleansing and the destruction of the flood, the Lord promises to Noah and his offspring a fresh start. After all Noah spent his Lent and his forty days on a boat with his family and every kind of animal and creature...forty days and forty nights. Often the church is compared to a boat and perhaps you have heard the saying that dates all the way back to the days of the early church comparing life in the church to Noah's ark: 'the stench inside would be unbearable if it weren't for the storm outside.' I don't think life together in Christian community is quite that stench-ridden, but we are certainly made up of imperfect and flawed people, people still trying to get it together, people still in process. It reminds me of the person who invited a neighbor to try out their church and the neighbor replied that they stayed away from churches because they were all so full of hypocrites, to which they person responded, 'well, there's always room for one more.' The hypocrites, after all are not just in here.

In fact, that's one problem or issue that always haunts me and puzzles me about this narrative about Noah and the flood... that somehow Noah and his descendants were preserved from destruction because of their virtue and their purity...it doesn't seem to be God's usual redemptive strategy. So Noah's Lenten challenge or Lenten discipline is basically to survive on this ark for forty days without losing his mind. And that is where we find him in chapter 9...recovering from the flood, giving thanks to God for preserving his life and receiving God's covenant to him and his descendants and all creation that 'never again shall all flesh be cut off by the waters of a flood, and never again shall there be a flood to destroy the earth.' And the Lord God even gives Noah a sign of this covenant to him and every living creature and all future generations: 'I have set my bow in the clouds over the earth and bow is seen in the clouds...when the bow is in the clouds, I will see it and remember the everlasting covenant between God and every living creature of all flesh that is on the earth' (Genesis 9: 11-16).

And so we can faithfully sing at the end of the arky song that at the 'end of the story, story, every-thing-is hunky, dory, dory, children of the Lord.' God cleanses the earth with this flood, God deals with evil, and God renews his covenant with creation. Life can start afresh. Humanity has a new life. Never will we get ourselves in such a mess again. But that is not where our passage ends. It doesn't end with everything hunky dory, it ends with Noah planting a vineyard, drinking too much wine, and embarrassing himself and his family in a very public way. This person who did everything he was commanded, this person who survived the flood, this person who heard God's new promise of a covenant and rainbow, this person cannot hold it together very long at all before it comes unraveling all around him.

Such dramatic reversals are only surprising to us if we have bought into the myth of human innocence and purity and the self-righteous delusion that we and Noah are basically good and getting better every day and the world out there and those who are not like us or disagree with us are basically evil and are our enemies. As Noah shows us in graphic detail, he and we and our world are more complicated than that and such news is shattering to those parts of us that still believe in human innocence and human perfectability. The historian Arthur Schlessinger reminds us that the great rags-to-riches steel magnate Andrew Carnegie once expressed such faith in the early part of the 20th century when celebrating the rise of humanity from lower to higher forms, declaring that there is no 'conceivable end to his march to perfection,' and echoing the thoughts of most intelligentsia, political scientists, and American elites of the time that proper education of individuals and reform of institutions would produce a near perfect human nature and society.¹⁶ Schlessinger then points us to the great American public theologian of the last century, Reinhold Niebuhr, who reminds us of our 'inability to comprehend the depth of evil to which individuals and communities may sink, particularly when they try to play the role of God to history.'¹⁷

Noah is set apart from all the others, saved from the flood, Noah survives the stench inside and the storm outside, and yet after all that, we come to see that Noah is no more virtuous and just as susceptible to impaired judgment as just about anyone else. There is a satirical religious website called the Babylon Bee and each day the put out a faux article that is funny but also insightful and usually playfully tweaking one or tweaking of our various religious traditions. This past week, there was an article that began with this headline: 'Confirmed: World Still Fallen.' And in a nutshell, that is the conclusion, I believe to this Noah narrative. There is the rainbow, the covenant, but also the confirmation that 'yep, the world is still fallen,' Noah is no angel, and we are not on the road to perfection.

It would be easy to end there…to say see we are all impaired, I'm not okay, you are not okay, and everything is going to hell in a hand basket. But while the journey we are on is not leading us to some realization of human perfection and human potential, it is also not leading us to a sense of complete despair and paralysis either. Noah is fruitful and does multiply…God's covenant continues to be offered to his creatures, to Israel, and finally to all humanity in Jesus Christ. Our condition may not always be or feel

---

[16] Arthur Schlessinger, 'Forgetting Reinhold Niebuhr,' in *The New York Times* Sunday Book Review, September 18, 2005.

[17] Arthur Schlessinger, 'Forgetting Reinhold Niebuhr,' in *The New York Times* Sunday Book Review, September 18, 2005.

ideal, but who and what Jesus Christ is calling us to be today as his church in this moment, while it will never be perfect or completely unhypocritical, it can also never be silent or worse, look the other way in the face of evil. There is power in resisting and there is purpose in working against the evils that plague us and our society. To paraphrase Reinhold Niebuhr again, none of the convictions of our faith contradict the need or the duty to try and do all we can to preserve our civilization. Our faith is in fact a prerequisite for helping save our civilization.[18] He was of course talking about the threats of Naziism and Communism in the middle of the 20th century that faced all Americans, but his words haunt us today in the aftermath of yet another school shooting by yet another impaired person who was able to attain yet another AR-15 semi-automatic assault rifle with relative ease. 'If we should perish,' Niebuhr writes, 'the ruthlessness of the foe would be only the secondary cause of the disaster. The primary cause would be that the strength of a giant nation was directed by eyes too blind to see all the hazards of the struggle; and the blindness would be induced not by some accident of nature or history but by (our) hatred and [our vanity].'[19]

We are mortal...we are impaired, and we are prone to vanity...as we heard this past Ash Wednesday, we are dust and to dust we shall return. But that is not all there is to us. Otherwise, our story would end with Noah's failed attempt at purity and human perfection. As Fleming Rutledge writes, 'there we remain unless there is an intervention from beyond this world order,' which is

---

[18] Arthur Schlessinger, 'Forgetting Reinhold Niebuhr,' in *The New York Times* Sunday Book Review, September 18, 2005.

[19] Reinhold Niebuhr, from 'The Irony of American History,' in Arthur Schlessinger, 'Forgetting Reinhold Niebuhr,' in *The New York Times* Sunday Book Review, September 18, 2005.

what we prepare for, reflect on, and look for during this forty day walk to the cross and God's intervention beyond it. And it is this power, that though we are impaired, this power refuses to allow us to accept the evils of our fallen world at face value as if they are inevitable and there is nothing we can do. And it is this power, that though we are impaired, refuses to allow us to look the other way. As Fleming Rutledge preached in a sermon in New York City at Grace Episcopal Church several years ago: 'the authors of scripture did not turn away from the unimaginable suffering of children. God the Father did not turn away. Jesus did not turn away…. only by attending to the horrors of this world,' only be facing them and confronting them 'can we continue to sing' and pray and believe that one day 'the agonies of the victims will someday be rectified, and the unconditional love of God in Jesus Christ will be the Last Word.'[20]

It is true that we live in a fallen world. Noah illustrates that in graphic detail. But Noah's failures and flaws are not the end or even the point of the story…nor is the story ever about our human potential or perfection. The miracle is that Noah's story continues in spite of the glaring flaws, God gives him the nerve to get up and continue to move forward with a sense of modesty about his abilities and a sense of contrition about his own capabilities for evil and vanity.[21] What Noah is not, is paralyzed, he is not paralyzed to accept his situation at face value, nor is he afraid, in spite of his limitations and his own flaws, to work to preserve his civilization and to multiply his children. May God give us the courage to do the same. Amen.

---

[20] Fleming Rutledge, 'Monsters at the Manger,' in *The Bible and the New York Times*, 59-60.

[21] Arthur Schlessinger, 'Forgetting Reinhold Niebuhr,' in *The New York Times* Sunday Book Review, September 18, 2005.

From Seeds to Weeds
Matthew 13:24-30

He put before them another parable: 'The kingdom of heaven may be compared to someone who sowed good seed in his field; but while everybody was asleep, an enemy came and sowed weeds among the wheat, and then went away. So when the plants came up and bore grain, then the weeds appeared as well. And the slaves of the householder came and said to him, "Master, did you not sow good seed in your field? Where, then, did these weeds come from?" He answered, "An enemy has done this." The slaves said to him, "Then do you want us to go and gather them?" But he replied, "No; for in gathering the weeds you would uproot the wheat along with them. Let both of them grow together until the harvest; and at harvest time I will tell the reapers, Collect the weeds first and bind them in bundles to be burned, but gather the wheat into my barn."'

For nearly three years, I worked as a Church of Scotland prison chaplain on a part-time basis. Most of our work was done during the week, but we would also lead Sunday services on a rotational basis about once a month. Sunday worship inside a prison is different in many ways than worship in sanctuary and church like this one. When we talk about freedom and freedom in Christ, it takes on a meaning inside a prison that it might not have when mentioned in worship here. It was also the one time in the prison that prisoners from all various units of the prison were allowed to come together for worship. One of the most powerful and fearful parts of the service for me was a part of the service that is also done here every week. It was the assurance of pardon after the prayer of confession when we are asked to confess our sins. One Sunday, I remember asking the question that is often asked in our confessional response, who is in a position to condemn? Just like here, usually there is just a pause and silence as we all realize that none of us can cast the first stone. But one Sunday, and honestly, I do not think this particular prisoner was trying to be a comedian or smart aleck, he was just blurting an answer out honestly, and when I asked who is in a position to condemn, he immediately answered right back, 'The magistrate.' And in his case, he had a point. The criminal judge had condemned him to serve a sentence, but in the case of the Christian faith, even the magistrate could not condemn him beyond that. But it was always in that part of the service, in a room full of criminals, thieves, addicts, violent offenders, and worse, it was these words that really got to me…'friends, hear the good news of the gospel, in Jesus Christ you are forgiven…in Jesus Christ we are forgiven.'

Now maybe those words pass over you each week and provide you comfort and assurance and a challenge to more fully embody the people in Jesus Christ that we already are and that we seek to become. But in the walls of the prison those words sounded more radical and powerful but also more fearful to me…hear the good news of the gospel, in Jesus Christ you are forgiven. I mean it is one thing to forgive the lady in the grocery store parking lot who hurled an expletive at us when we inadvertently took her parking spot or to ask God forgiveness for saying something hurtful or unnecessary to a friend or neighbor, but to believe that forgiveness is possible and given by Jesus Christ beyond our small blunders, flaws, and imperfections takes us to a world beyond our own comfort level and notions of reasonableness. It was not always a comfortable feeling to look out over a congregation of prisoners and declare to them that in Christ, their sins were forgiven. What exactly, I wanted to know, standing there with some fresh drips of perspiration, was being forgiven? Forgiveness is just for little stuff, right?

In the Meantime

In a sermon preached to prisoners sixty years ago, theologian Karl Barth criticized depictions of the crucifixion that leave out the fact Jesus was on the cross with two criminals hanging on either side of him. The two thieves, he reminds us, must not be left out, because as Luke 23:33 tells us, 'they crucified him with criminals, one on either side of him.' Barth goes on to say, in a way that sounds a bit outlandish, that Jesus on the cross with the two criminals (one who responds to him and one who rejects him by the way) is the first Christian community. They are 'the first certain, indissoluble and indestructible Christian community,' because they are a gathering of human beings with Jesus in the midst of them who are directly affected by his life, his words of assurance, and bear witness to his faithfulness and all that he does for them. To be the in the presence of such promise and live by it, Barth believes, is to be a Christian community and he makes the point that the first Christian community was made up of two thieves.[22]

So what do we have to say to that? Maybe it makes us feel better about our own prospects? Maybe it helps us to see the church differently as well…not as a place where there are no weeds or impurities, but as a place where in spite of it God is able to shine through and break through and produce a vision of his kingdom at work among us, through us, and in spite of us. After all, that is how our scripture lesson and this parable begins is it not? The kingdom of heaven is like someone who sowed good seed in his field and allowed weeds to grow among the wheat. Why not just spray round-up on everything, his servants ask? Why not send us out there to take care of the problems and fix everything, they want to know? Don't you know your whole operation and purpose are going to be destroyed? But the seed sower is insistent and commands them to let the weeds be grown alongside the good

---

[22] Karl Barth, 'The Criminals With Him,' in *Deliverance to the Captives*, 77.

fruit…otherwise going in there to rid all the evil might do damage to the good harvest or destroy it all together. Let it grow together and at harvest time, the weeds and wheat can be sorted out and dealt with. This is what the kingdom of God is like even if we have a hard time making sense of it.

For too long I think we have been quick to read ourselves right into this parable as the good seed…trying to do our best but held back by evildoers or the evil of the world outside of us…well they'll finally get their comeuppance at the final harvest, we think. Or perhaps we have too quickly seen ourselves as the weeds…beating ourselves up about our evil ways or believing we have to attain a certain level of goodness or we'll be cast out. But listen to the parable: the kingdom of God is like someone who sowed good seed in a field but let the wheat and the weeds grow together before sifting it out…could God's encounters with us be much more like this kingdom than we realize? Might the good seed and the weeds often grow up together in us and with us God patiently waits to sift and filter and refine us Sunday after Sunday until his kingdom comes? Like that first Christian community of criminals at the cross, might we be a mixed bag ourselves, might we at times be both deniers and faithful responders, might it only be possible for God to extract and coax any faithfulness and joy and goodness out of us by allowing the weeds to grow there too…whether it come in the form of selfishness or greed or our rolodex of self-destructive tendencies.

We really know very little about those two criminals crucified with Jesus…they are often forgotten or at least airbrushed away or made to fade to the background of the crucifixion. In his sermon to prisoners, Karl Barth reminds us that 'we know nothing about their lives, of their misdoings and crimes. We do not know whether they could plead (extenuating) circumstances, or whether their guilt was even greater than we may think.' And yet, no one has been closer, Barth reminds us, than they to God's act of reconciliation and redemption of the world. These two weeds who are not too tangled up or forsaken but are invited to participate in Christ's redemption of the world. Barth reminds us that Jesus died for these two criminals who were crucified with him....that he 'did not die for the sake of a good world, he died for the sake of an evil world, (he did not die) for the pious, but for the godless, not for the just, but for the unjust, for the deliverance, the victory and joy of all, that they might have life.[23] The wheat and the weeds grow together. In us. And in each other.

The reformer Martin Luther, who in various ways we are commemorating in this 500th year of the Reformation that some of his actions initiated, Luther had a term for our condition. In Latin, it was called *simul iustus et peccator*, meaning we are at the same time justified and a sinner. We are never just one or the other, but always both at the same time and at all times, we are simultaneously weed and wheat. It would be nice at times to live in a world of starker contrasts...to say for sure who is in and who is out...to say with certainty we are on the always on the side of the angels and they (them out there) are on always on the side of evil. We are the good wheat and they are the bad wheat. But it is hard for me to believe that God would become flesh and preach in parables and go to the trouble of dying on the cross with criminals just to tell us that kind of news. Instead, we find ourselves, more happily I think, with a lot sketchier resumes, full of weeds and roguish behavior we just can't shake loose of...but in the hands of a Savior who can sift through 99 weeds to find our 1 good seed, a Savior who lets the weeds and wheat grow together in us, because he knows there is

---

[23] Karl Barth, 'The Criminals With Him,' in *Deliverance to the Captives*, 81.

some residue, some reflection, some harvest of his kingdom in every last one of us. Amen.

More Than a Feeling
1 John 4:7-21

Beloved, let us love one another, because love is from God; everyone who loves is born of God and knows God. Whoever does not love does not know God, for God is love. God's love was revealed among us in this way: God sent his only Son into the world so that we might live through him. In this is love, not that we loved God but that he loved us and sent his Son to be the atoning sacrifice for our sins. Beloved, since God loved us so much, we also ought to love one another. No one has ever seen God; if we love one another, God lives in us, and his love is perfected in us. By this we know that we abide in him and he in us, because he has given us of his Spirit. And we have seen and do testify that the Father has sent his Son as the Savior of the world. God abides in those who confess that Jesus is the Son of God, and they abide in God. So we have known and believe the love that God has for us. God is love, and those who abide in love abide in God, and God abides in them. Love has been perfected among us in this: that we may have boldness on the day of judgment, because as he is, so are we in this world. There is no fear in love, but perfect love casts out fear; for fear has to do with punishment, and whoever fears has not reached perfection in love. We love[a] because he first loved us. Those who say, "I love God," and hate their brothers or sisters, are liars; for those who do not love a brother or sister whom they have seen, cannot love God whom they have not seen. The commandment we have from him is this: those who love God must love their brothers and sisters also.

Such a simple command. All we need to do now is cue the Beatles, who remind us that love, love, love is all we need. It's easy. I love the song and I really, really wish it were true or at least I wish it were easy. But we only have to go from the Beatles to Sigmund

Freud to get a sense that love, if it is anything more than an amorphous sentimental feeling, is anything but easy. New Testament scholar Susan Eastman reminds us that though Freud was no fan of Christianity, he shares these insights about Christian love: 'The commandment, 'Love they neighbor as thyself,' writes Freud, 'is the strongest defense there is against human aggressiveness and it is a superlative example of the unpsychological proceedings of the cultural superego. The commandment is impossible to fulfill; such an enormous inflation of love can only lower its value and not remedy the difficulty (that) anyone who follows such a precept in modern-day civilization only puts himself at a disadvantage vis-à-vis the person who disregards it.'[24]

So though I really like their song, not only are the Beatles wrong about love being easy, but love may not even be in our best self-interest and may in fact put as at a disadvantage if our neighbor chooses to get the upper hand and take advantage. 'All you need is love, love, love is all you need.' Let's see if we can put the Beatles and Freud in conversation together. Here goes: 'love is all you need if you want to be put at a disadvantage toward your human competition, love is all you need if you want to be taken advantage of, love is all you need if you like losing the fight or the argument or the upper hand. Love, love, love. We started with the theology and philosophy of the Beatles and found it somewhat wanting, then we moved on to the theology and philosophy of Sigmund Freud and perhaps found it a bit too cynical and sordid for our more noble ideals. Perhaps we ought to end with Forrest Gump who does not gush with eloquent lyrics about love or dismiss at is a

---

[24] Sigmund Freud, *Civilization and Its* Discontents trans. James Strachey (New York: Norton, 1962), 90, in Susan Grove Eastman, 'Love's Folly: Love and Knowledge in I Corinthians,' *from Interpretation: A Journal of Bible and Theology*, 16.

fool's errand, but just declares to his lifelong mate Jenny that he knows what love is. From the Beatles to Freud to Forrest Gump, do we know what love is?

'It is somewhat amusing to me that some of the most often read 'love' passages in scripture, I Corinthians 13 and this passage in 1 John, were both written to communities in serious conflict. Neither Paul's words to the Corinthians about clanging cymbals and noisy gongs, about love being patient and kind and not envious or boastful or arrogant or rude, neither Paul's words nor John's words to the Johannine community that comprise our scripture lesson today, were written in a 'kum ba yah moment' of wedding bliss or group togetherness. The Corinthians were fractured and splintering into factions around various leaders, certain members were flaunting and taunting members who in their minds had lesser gifts. Wealthier members were bringing lavish meals to eat in worship while poorer members could only watch in envy and get their only nourishment from the bread and cup of communion. And John's words about love were not written in some romantic moment of inspiration or some wedding planner's dream but were also written in the midst of a fractured and splintering community in which some members denied that Jesus was the 'Messiah' or 'Christ' and others could not conceive of a deity or a 'Christ' who would sully himself by becoming a human being. These beautiful words of love come to us and encounter us almost as if they are cracked open out of these conflicts and broken communities. Smooth sailing and superficial togetherness could never have elicited or produced such a description of what love looks like and what love is.

In a recent article in *The Christian Century*, Jason Micheli reads the various post-Easter accounts and wonders aloud why in nearly all gospel accounts the common behavioral trait that always seems to befit the disciples in the presence of the resurrected Christ is one of fear. Why are they always afraid, even after Jesus visits them a third time, in some cases? It is not because they are having a hard time believing or even that they cannot quite get their minds around the resurrection, rather he argues, that it is Jesus' resurrection and return that strikes fear in them. 'They know their scripture, and they know they've abandoned Jesus. They've denied ever knowing him. They've turned tail, turned a blind eye, washed their hands of his blood. They've scapegoated him into suffering and stood silently by while others mocked him and taunted him. They've let the world sin all its sins into him and then left him forsaken on a cross.'[25] If Jesus is raised from the dead, then they know what is next. Revenge. Time to settle scores. Time to get them back.

But what Micheli reminds us is that the resurrection is shocking to the disciples because Christ does not come back to indict them or condemn them or make them pay the wages of their fickleness and abandonment and cowardice. 'He spares them the everlasting judgment and shame they had every reason' to expect.[26] They don't know what love is, until it stands among them in their fear and trembling and embraces them and invites them to table fellowship. They don't know what love is, or at least what they thought was love is completely turned upside down and redefined by a Savior whose love 'bears all things, believes all things, hopes all things, endures all things, and never ends,' in pursuit of these frightened human beings (I Corinthians 13:7-8). We love, not because we can concoct or get in touch with some deep sentimental sensation deep

---

[25] Jason Micheli, 'Easter is not Good News without the Cross,' in *The Christian Century*, https://www.christiancentury.org/blog-post/ccblogs-network/easter-not-good-news-without-cross

[26] Jason Micheli, 'Easter is not Good News without the Cross,' in *The Christian Century*, https://www.christiancentury.org/blog-post/ccblogs-network/easter-not-good-news-without-cross

inside of ourselves, we love, John tells us, when all bets are off, when it is all hitting the fan, in the midst of fear and abandonment, and when there is nothing to agree with or be attracted to in our neighbor. We love, not because we are good at it or experts or superior beings; we love, because God first loved us, because God does not settle for anything less than a people and a community who embody such stubborn, persistent, and unending love.

This past week I had the opportunity to hear a fellow colleague in ministry speak about her own call to ministry that came to her when her young husband was dying of cancer and she was trying to be a mother to a year-old baby. What a strange time for the risen Christ to show up in her life and pursue her, but upon reflecting back upon that experience, she said that what she learned through a very low and difficult time in her life was that while the powers of scientific advancements and medical treatments were limited, the power of God's grace was inexhaustible. Love never ends. We love, because God first loved us and whether we can at all times see it, touch it, feel it, or experience it, we are held and pursued and on the way toward a cruciform love that 'bears all things, believes all things, and hopes all things.' Even when we think we deserve less or that love is something easier. Even when we think we are unworthy or unfit. Even in the depths of life's struggles. Christ's love has a way of entering in, embracing us, and sending us off in a better direction.

Part II: Meantime

Nothing but Prodigals
Ephesians 2:1-10

> *You were dead through the trespasses and sins in which you once lived, following the course of this world, following the ruler of the power of the air, the spirit that is now at work among those who are disobedient. All of us once lived among them in the passions of our flesh, following the desires of flesh and senses, and we were by nature children of wrath, like everyone else. But God, who is rich in mercy, out of the great love with which he loved us even when we were dead through our trespasses, made us alive together with Christ—by grace you have been saved—and raised us up with him and seated us with him in the heavenly places in Christ Jesus, so that in the ages to come he might show the immeasurable riches of his grace in kindness toward us in Christ Jesus. For by grace you have been saved through faith, and this is not your own doing; it is the gift of God— not the result of works, so that no one may boast. For we are what he has made us, created in Christ Jesus for good works, which God prepared beforehand to be our way of life.'*

It can be easy to miss out on the radicalness of Paul's letter to the Ephesians and the shock value of his theological proclamations throughout the New Testament; we dilute them into church speak and religious exhortations. But what Paul is telling the Ephesians has happened in Jesus Christ has altered the normal course of the universe, and that all of us, every last one of us, were destined for destruction and disarray and turmoil, but God, who is rich in mercy, even while we were dead through our trespasses, has intervened and made us alive through Jesus Christ. 'By grace you have been saved,' Paul declares. 'And this is not your own doing.' This is not humdrum church-speak. This is radical. And his sounds like great news…almost too good to be true.

Perhaps you are not all that surprised about this, but we ministers of the gospel and people of the cloth are just as gifted as anyone in the practice of sin, and without a lot of help and encouragement, we can trespass ourselves into quite a bit of trouble. So it was that I encountered a recent article about a local pastor at a well-known church who was arrested recently on drug charges and drug possession. I had an immediate knee-jerk reaction, once I made sure and gave thanks that the church was not a Presbyterian one, but my immediate reaction, somewhat smugly and self-satisfyingly, was to launch right into the prayer of the Pharisee: 'Thank you, Lord, that I am not as other people.' Thank you that I am not like that guy or the phrase comes to mind that is actually not in the Bible but most likely originated with the English expression uttered as prisoners were being led to the scaffold in the 16th century, 'There but for the grace of God, go I.' Perhaps it is just part of our human nature and our piety to pray aloud or in our heart of hearts, 'Yes, Lord, I know I'm not perfect, but at least I am not THAT bad.' We are very skilled and clever and quite artful at differentiating ourselves from others or assuring ourselves or others with the false sense of security that 'while I may not be able to preach the birds out of the trees,' and 'while the sermon last week may have been a dud, at least I'm not making those kind of headlines,' or at least I am not that kind of sinner. 'Thank you Lord, that I am not as other people.'

Our recent guest Fleming Rutledge, who is very deft at disclosing crucial provocative material from Paul's letters, reminds us that Ephesians, not to mention the biblical narrative in general, puts before us a very different view of human nature. She reminds us that 'there is a sense in which we are offered no loopholes, no escape hatches whatsoever,' and that Jesus did not teach to pray, 'Lord I did my best,' or 'Lord, at least I'm not like that guy,' but rather he taught us to pray the prayer, 'God be merciful to me a sinner.'²⁷ In his letter to the church at Rome, Paul reminds that congregation that 'there is no one righteous, no, not one,' (Romans 3:10) and that there is not only no distinction in Christ between male and female, slave and free, Jew and Gentile, there are no degrees of goodness/badness, and that 'there is no distinction; all have sinned and fall short of the glory of God (Romans 3:22-23).' Rutledge goes on to remind us that each one of us are distinguished 'by our failure to embody our human potential and to mirror the glory of God,' and that 'even the greatest saints' and those 'we admire most are the first to admit this.' To put it another way, if there are statues of any of us now or in the future, they all really deserve to be pulled down, some more than others perhaps, but we all fail to reach our potential and reflect God's grace, each in our own spectacular ways.

Fleming Rutledge recounts the dialogue she heard on a busy New York City street from 'one upper-crust, three-piece-suited man' saying to another, angrily, 'my son-in-law is an emotional cripple!' To which the other man responded quietly, 'We're all emotional cripples.'²⁸ Or hear it from Paul: 'For by grace you have been saved through faith, and this is not your own doing; it is the gift of God,' not the result of something you did or something you have been able to achieve, but because in spite of the fact that we are flawed and do not ever want to identify with the worst in ourselves or others, God has made us into new creations in Christ, and we have been saved from ever having to prove our worth before God or from ever having to believe that there is a shortcut to redemption from which we are exempt. 'I'm bad, but not that bad.' To which Paul tells the Ephesians, all of us were dead to our sins, none of us should be able to pray 'Thank you Lord that I am not as other

---

27 Fleming Rutledge, 'The Man With No Trousers,' in *The Undoing of Death*, 104.

28 Fleming Rutledge, 'The Man With No Trousers,' in *The Undoing of Death*, 104.

people,' but to see ourselves as we truly are. To see ourselves as God sees us, and as God chooses to see us, is to pray the prayer, 'God be merciful to me a sinner.'

Our sermon text comes from Ephesians, not the prodigal son passage in Luke, but Paul tells the Ephesians that all of us, in our own way, are prodigal sons and daughters and that there is no other way home except for God's grace to find us. No other way home for us but through the prodigal Son, who leaves his homeland and his Father and enters into our muck and our messes but does not leave us there or where we are, but instead leads us back home, prodigals all. Not because we are a superior community, or better behaved than most. Not because we are loved by God any more than the next person, or because we are any less or more flawed and sinful than the next person. No, Paul says, it is by grace you have been saved…not by your own doing…not by your resume…not because you are little better or higher achieving than the person to the right or to the left of you…none of us is going to stand up well if that is how the score is tallied. Rather God has intervened radically in Jesus Christ and all of us who were destined for disobedience and destruction and disarray, have instead been saved, made new creatures in Christ. We are miraculously seen differently from God's vantage point because Christ has wedged himself between us and God and refused to let us be anything more or less than covered up by his grace.

So we can continue and probably will continue at times to have bouts of sizing ourselves up, comparing ourselves to others out there or placing our trust in our ability 'to not be as bad as' fill in the blank. It is possible to live our entire lives keeping score and believing that our virtues and human potential will ultimately be enough to save us or make us whole. 'Lord, I thank you that I am at least better than that rabble...but there is another way right before us...and it is one that has come to terms with the reality that God loves rabble, that in Christ God becomes rabble, and that through Christ God refuses to see any of us as rabble. Not one. I realize our day-to-day lives often have a different trajectory and that the Pharisees' prayer can feel more comfortable and fitting to get through the day. But even when we find ourselves praying thus and seeing our world and each other in such black and white, good and bad, us and them ways, Paul is pointing to a living Savior in our midst who refuses to draw such conclusions about us for the time being. The wheat and the chaff remain together—sometimes right inside of us, and Christ seems more than willing to die in order that no such divisions, distinctions, or pecking orders remain our way of life or stay with us forever, no more Jew and Gentile, slave and free, male and female. None of us is meant for destruction...and as Paul reminds us, 'We are what God has made us, created in Christ for good works, which God prepared beforehand to be our way of life.' So whether we are self-satisfied or struggling mightily or somewhere else in the pecking order this day, that is not the ultimate reality. It is to become what we already are in Christ Jesus our Lord. Amen.

Plying the Church's Trade
Matthew 18:15-20

'If another member of the church sins against you, go and point out the fault when the two of you are alone. If the member listens to you, you have regained that one. But if you are not listened to, take one or two others along with you, so that every word may be confirmed by the evidence of two or three witnesses. If the member refuses to listen to them, tell it to the church; and if the offender refuses to listen even to the church, let such a one be to you as a Gentile and a tax-collector. Truly I tell you, whatever you bind on earth will be bound in heaven, and whatever you loose on earth will be loosed in heaven. Again, truly I tell you, if two of you agree on earth about anything you ask, it will be done for you by my Father in heaven. For where two or three are gathered in my name, I am there among them.'

It is an old joke and it is not an original joke…but here goes: you've heard about the American Christian who was shipwrecked and stranded on a desert island. Like Tom Hanks in the movie Castaway, he spent some time trying to get rescued and was finally able to signal to an airplane or boat and they sent a rescue helicopter to pick him up. The helicopter landed alongside the beach, loaded up the rescue-ee, and took off for safety and home. As the helicopter was flying away, both rescuers and rescue-ee looked back on the little island where he had made his temporary home and shelter. Along the beach there were three huts. And the rescuers asked the rescued person what the first hut was: that was his home…where he slept and took shelter and made his meals. What was the second hut? That was his church…where he worshiped and prayed and sang God's praises. Well what's the third hut his rescuer asked? That is the church I used to go to, he explained.

Community is hard…even when we are off by ourselves. Even then, we are not at peace with ourselves and flail at practicing community. Will Willimon explains it this way: 'you see, I'm not a 'community person' by natural inclination. Tell me I have some charismatic flair for leadership. Praise me for the art of my preaching or the empathy of my pastoral care, just let me share myself and pour out my feelings, urge me to become a spiritual virtuoso, but please do not yoke me to the Body, do not marry me to that unruly Bride, do not force me to find what I do and therefore who I am among those who gather at my so very mundane congregation.'[29]

If another member of the church sins against you…this is where Jesus begins talking about Christian community…not in terms of beautiful moments of togetherness and spiritual ecstasy…not in terms of setting the world straight and getting all the world's problems sorted out…not in terms of a gathering of people who have it all together or who are really nice and kind and have superior spiritual gifts…no, Jesus begins talking about the Christian community as a place where sinners gather. 'If another member of the church sins against you.' He assumes us to be a church of sinners.

The first congregation I served was in a small hamlet of about five hundred people in the coastal farmland of eastern North Carolina. The town center consisted of a post office, a town hall, a sheriff's substation, and medical supply business, railroad tracks right

---

[29] William H. Willimon, 'The Spiritual Formation of the Pastor,' in *the Pastor's Guide to Personal Spiritual Formation*, 25.

through the middle of the town, a volunteer fire department, and an old building that had been a hardware store, but was vacant, empty, and kind of an eye-sore (it has since burned down and collapsed). This building presented a conundrum to the pastor nominating committee…how can we interest someone in this call to ministry with this vacant/less than charming building sitting right in the middle of our town? Should we avoid it on our tours? Should we not draw attention to it? Should we mention it at all? Finally, one of the matriarchs of the congregation who was serving on the pastor nominating committee spoke up and said, 'I want you to drive him right in front of that building. I don't want you to pretend that it is not there or try to avoid it…we need to show him and his wife who we are, warts and all." And that is exactly what they did…and they got a new pastor with his own sinful baggage, warts and all.

But isn't it interesting that one of the few times in scripture that Jesus addresses the Christian community and who we are and what it means to be a part of the church, he assumes that we are sinners. Now when one of you sins against the other, here is how you handle it. He assumes we are not pristine or completely functional or perfect in every way…his interest, he tells us in Luke, is not in the 99 righteous persons, but in the one sinner[30] and that who he expects to find and minister to such folk in the Christian community that belongs to him. So we can engage with and read this passage from Matthew as some kind of step by step formula for how to confront someone who commits an offense against us (and in some way it does function for this purpose), but perhaps more deeply, practicing forgiveness is not so much a step by step skill to be honed or a human achievement and accomplishment as

---

[30] Luke 15:7

it is a way of life,[31] a way of being, a reality and community that we are baptized into and with whom we struggle and seek to live with and try to forgive, warts and all. 'When another member of the church, sins against you…'

Living as a community of forgiveness and reconciliation, is a way of life and continually pursuing reconciliation will encompass all our life and life together. It is not just for moments where we feel someone has sinned against us, but it is a way of being with one another and how together we help each other see our world. I am not sure where this prayer originated, but a prayer that we as a staff use from time to time to remind us of who we are, begins like this: 'Heavenly Father, help us to remember that the jerk who cut us off in traffic last night is a single mother who worked nine hours that day and is rushing home to cook dinner, help with homework, do the laundry, and spend a few precious moments with her children, or that they old couple walking annoyingly slow through the store aisles and blocking our shopping progress are savoring this moment, knowing that based on the biopsy report she got last week, this will be the last year they go shopping together.'[32]

How does Jesus begin again? When another member of the church sins against you…we are a not a community of pure people or spiritual virtuosos or world-beating Christians…we are a community of sinners trying to receive ourselves and others as God's forgiven children, trying to give and receive forgiveness in all realms of our lives. This week the University of First Presbyterian Church is hosting a civility workshop to address diminishing where the social capital for our society and relationships and politics.

---

[31] Thomas W. Currie, 'I Believe in the forgiveness of sins,' *The Presbyterian Outlook*, 13.

[32] 'Help Us to Remember,' author unknown.

There is little civility for each other and especially those who 'sin' against us because they do not see the world as we do. While civility is not the exact same thing as practicing forgiveness or reconciliation, practicing civility and treating each other with respect and dignity is exactly what Jesus' instructions in Matthew are about. It is not about the Christian community seeking to be holier than thou or giving each other a laundry list of faults and presenting them to one another with 2 or 3 others along for the ride. Rather, we disagree, we sin against each other, we malfunction and mess up, we see each other's warts, and yet such a life unfolds, begins and ends in a community where correction and opposition and forgiveness occur within a context of love so confident and joyous that it rejoices as it tries to forgive.

Recently Samuel Wells who serves the St. Martin-in-the-Fields parish in London told about a difficult 11-year-old boy from his first pastoral appointment who started coming to his church and who was difficult in every regard: bullying younger children, telling off the adults, unwilling to accept much in terms of direction or discipline. Yet nine months later, in spite of the challenges he presented that little church, the boy became baptized into that congregation and made his profession of faith by thanking those in the congregation who did not throw him out after that first weekend. Recently, Wells had the opportunity to catch up with the young man, now an adult, who has made a life for himself and who had kept a scrapbook of those moments he cherished in which that church and its priest ministered to him. Wells summarizes his reflection by reflecting out loud, 'we gave you some small moments of love and forbearance, but you—you showed us forgiveness and resurrection; in short, the gospel. How can we ever thank you?'[33]

Jesus assumes we are sinners...that is where he begins...that is where we begin...but that is not where our passage ends is it? It ends not with a problem or a conflict or a procedure, but it ends with hope. 'Where two or three are gathered in my name, I am there among them.' May we find ourselves there too, unwilling to keep track of petty slights, sinful failures, and those sins against us, as we offer ourselves up to the One who forgives us even as he is affixed to a cross. May we find him and ourselves there too...at the community of the cross, where sinners gather...where forgiveness is practiced...where Jesus finds and defines the church...where we become our true selves. Amen.

---

[33] Samuel Wells, 'Love Becomes Fruitful' in *The Christian Century* (September 13, 2017), 35.

How am I doing?
Romans 6:1-11

What are supposed to do with our lives? Keep on sinning since we know God's grace abounds for us? You know we've all thought that, and the refreshing news is that we are not the first or the last to wonder such things. As we heard in Romans 5 last week, Christ's death and life with us has placed us in a grace that we do not deserve, grace we could never earn, and a grace that we can ignore and struggle with and run from but never lose. The Reformer Martin Luther once compared our reception of grace to a cow standing in front of a wide-open gate looking puzzled...we think it is too good to be true...we think there must be a catch...we cannot imagine such fortunate circumstances. Here in Romans 6, Paul is sharing in that wonder and also trying to describe and exhort and instruct the Christian community in Rome and us about how we were to live in such a state of grace. Listen for the Word of God from Paul's letter to the Romans, chapter 6, reading at the first verse.

> *What then are we to say? Should we continue in sin in order that grace may abound? By no means! How can we who died to sin go on living in it? Do you not know that all of us who have been baptized into Christ Jesus were baptized into his death? Therefore, we have been buried with him by baptism into death, so that, just as Christ was raised from the dead by the glory of the Father, so we too might walk in newness of life. For if we have been united with him in a death like his, we will certainly be united with him in a resurrection like his. We know that our old self was crucified with him so that the body of sin might be destroyed, and we might no longer be enslaved to sin. For whoever has died is freed from sin. But if we have died with Christ, we believe that we will also*

live with him. We know that Christ, being raised from the dead, will never die again; death no longer has dominion over him. The death he died, he died to sin, once for all; but the life he lives, he lives to God. So you also must consider yourselves dead to sin and alive to God in Christ Jesus.

Rumor has it that Ed Koch, the once popular mayor of New York City during the 1980s, used to campaign and make rounds throughout his constituency during election time, asking one simple question: 'How am I doing?' How-m-I doing?' Isn't that what it means to be a Christian in a nutshell. To take inventory, to measure our growth and see where we are lacking or in need of self-improvement, and then to go about trying to grow and become a better person, a better Christian, to have more faith. I remember once when we had our first baby on the way and we are purchasing a new car that would be safe and accommodating for a growing family. When we were trying to finance the car and I was sweating and hemming and hawing and the gentleman helping us found out I was a minister, he told me I just needed a little more faith. I told him that I did not think that kind of faith was going to produce a larger down payment, but that is what we think the Christian life is good for mainly …increasing our levels of faith, filling us out spiritually, helping us become better at life. That is often how we tend to think about the spiritual life or what we mean by sanctification or spiritual growth in the Christian life. And there is a part of that that makes a lot of sense…who wants to make the effort to get everyone out of bed, get everyone as spit and polished as we are able, make the effort to scramble to church on a Sunday morning, only to find out that scripture is somewhat ambivalent about whether or not there will be a tangible reward for all your efforts.

In an interview about a decade ago with Eugene Peterson he explained the predicament this way: "one way to define spiritual life is getting so tired and fed up with yourself you go on to something better, which is following Jesus. But the minute we start advertising faith in terms of benefits, we're just exacerbating the self problem. 'With Christ, you're better, stronger, more likeable, you enjoy some ecstasy.' But's just more self,' Peterson reminds us. He continues: 'We've all met a certain type of spiritual person. She's a wonderful person. She loves the Lord. She prays and reads the Bible all the time. But all she thinks about is herself. She's not a selfish person. But she's always at the center of everything she's doing. 'How can I witness better? How can I do this better? How can I take care of this person's problem better? It's (still) me, me, me disguised in a way that is difficult to see because her spiritual talk disarms us.'[34]

In other words, perhaps the most profound spiritual moment of our lives occurs when we stop asking or worrying about 'how we are doing' in terms of faith or the spiritual life or how we measure up spiritually to others. I think that is the life of faith Paul is trying to describe with us in Romans chapter 6. Yes, we are self-destructive, yes even when we try to do something good it is often tainted by our ulterior motives, and yes humanity as a whole is even worse. We are constantly picking on each other, oppressing each other, starting unprovoked wars and rightly deserve death and destruction and yet Paul tells us that Christ willingly enters into what we deserve, death, destruction, sin and emptiness, entering into our rightful place, and carries it all away. That is the grace in which we now stand, so to be a Christian is not to try to inflate ourselves into better people, but to daily die and rise with Christ, to daily see that we have been liberated from trying to prove our

---

[34] Eugene Peterson, 'Spirituality for All the Wrong Reasons,' *Christianity Today* (March 2005), 45.

worth or improve ourselves. Our old self, Paul tells us in verse 6, has been extinguished in the death of Jesus Christ and we are already a new creature in Christ, born out of Christ's resurrection, loved by God, and free to live joyfully. As new creatures in Christ, we come to terms with the news that Christ is risen and that in him and with him we are too. In Christ's dying and rising, Paul proclaims, we have already been made a new creation and the point of life is learning how to become what we already are in Jesus Christ; people who attend to the need of the moment, people who do not worry too much about whether or not they measure up or have enough faith, people who have become self-forgetful, and who hope to die to ourselves and be resurrected to reflect something of the grace of Jesus Christ. For the person who wants to find seven easy steps to becoming a good Christian in the self-improvement section of Barnes and Noble, such news may confound and perplex us. For the Christian who is used to living a more or less virtuous and balanced lifestyle, Paul's words to the Romans might strike us as too abstract, not practical or applicable enough when all we think we are after is a little bit of linear growth and another installment of self-help religion.

Theologian Karl Barth even challenges us further. In a sermon to prisoners in the Basel jail entitled 'You May,' he stated that the most dangerous human response to God's grace is to believe we can do justice to what is demanded of us in the Christian life. Thinking that we can build a bridge of our own 'goodness, virtue, righteousness, and piety' that stretches closer to God gives us the false illusion that we can confront God as an equal and that the point of our lives is to find ways in which God can 'recognize us, praise, reward us, as we obviously deserve.'[35]

---

[35] Karl Barth *Call for God*, 22.

What then are we to say---Paul hauntingly and tauntingly asks us at the beginning of our lesson. Should we just keep on sinning in order that God's grace may surround us all the more? How should we live our lives? Not by constantly conducting a self-assessment of our level of spiritual worth or faith or by constantly checking our spiritual temperature. Instead, we learn to die to our self-seeking ways and to trust that in each given moment, God will raise us to shine as the people we truly are, dying and rising with Christ, starting again each day, and losing ourselves in the task or the song or the person before us.

How am I doing? How are we doing? We already know the answer...Paul makes it very clear to us in the last verse, verse 11 of our reading. Miraculously Christ lives and because he lives, we must consider ourselves dead to sin and alive to God in Christ Jesus.

Lost in freedom, lost in love, and lost in joy, we get to spend the rest of our lives seeking to become the people we already are in Jesus Christ our Lord. Amen.

A Hot Mess
Matthew 27:11-26

Now Jesus stood before the governor; and the governor asked him, "Are you the King of the Jews?" Jesus said, "You say so." But when he was accused by the chief priests and elders, he did not answer. Then Pilate said to him, "Do you not hear how many accusations they make against you?" But he gave him no answer, not even to a single charge, so that the governor was greatly amazed.

Now at the festival the governor was accustomed to release a prisoner for the crowd, anyone whom they wanted. At that time they had a notorious prisoner, called Jesus Barabbas. So after they had gathered, Pilate said to them, "Whom do you want me to release for you, Jesus Barabbas or Jesus who is called the Messiah?" For he realized that it was out of jealousy that they had handed him over. While he was sitting on the judgment seat, his wife sent word to him, "Have nothing to do with that innocent man, for today I have suffered a great deal because of a dream about him." Now the chief priests and the elders persuaded the crowds to ask for Barabbas and to have Jesus killed. The governor again said to them, "Which of the two do you want me to release for you?" And they said, "Barabbas." Pilate said to them, "Then what should I do with Jesus who is called the Messiah?" All of them said, "Let him be crucified!" Then he asked, "Why, what evil has he done?" But they shouted all the more, "Let him be crucified!"

So when Pilate saw that he could do nothing, but rather that a riot was beginning, he took some water and washed his hands before the crowd, saying, "I am innocent of this man's blood; see to it yourselves." Then the people as a whole answered, "His blood be on us and on our children!" So he released Barabbas for them; and after flogging Jesus, he handed him over to be crucified.

According to the Oxford dictionary, a hot mess is 'a person or thing that is spectacularly unsuccessful or disordered, especially one that is a source of peculiar fascination.' We've already contributed to the hot mess atmosphere, parading in here with palm branches, I even saw a few Presbyterians waving them. We have participated in the triumphal and celebratory entry, we've been pierced by the voice of the tenor announcing the arrival of Jesus on the donkey. But there is much more to this story than a parade. Hear again how the last words of our scripture lesson read: 'and Pilate handed him over to be crucified.' From parade to crucifixion…all in one passage. Hot mess indeed.

Not long ago, I was speaking to a member of the church who was celebrating the end of the work week and reminding me that it was finally Friday…the beginning of the weekend…the two days off…time to unwind and leave work early. I reminded her that for the minister, Friday is not as exciting. The anxiety level begins to build on Friday and for those who impose an end of the week deadline for completion of the sermon, if it is not done by Friday at 5:00 p.m., one's mood can turn anxious, cranky, fidgety, and a bit short fused. Many years ago, I read a reflection Frederick Buechner wrote from the perspective of Pontius Pilate and in it he speculated that Pontius Pilate had a big weekend planned; a barbecue with friends coming into town for the Passover weekend. So throughout the interchange between Jesus and Pilate in our lesson today maybe Pilate is just trying to get to the weekend, perhaps we can hear him singing as background music to our passage that it is 5 o'clock somewhere. He is tired of playing political football with the chief priests and the crowds and the Roman bureaucracy on this holiday weekend. He is not going to let this hot mess ruin his weekend; he has friends coming over; his wife is weighing in and weighing on him about being involved with this guy Jesus at all, and the last thing he needs is a politically, religiously, and socially charged situation wrecking his special plans. He washes his hands of the situation, frees Barabbas, gives the fickle crowds what they want, and refuses to allow this hot mess to destroy his weekend.

Everything about this Palm Sunday entry and this encounter with Pilate fits our definition: raucous and disorderly crowds from the parade to the angry mob gathered in front of the courthouse; disturbed and in over their head religious and political leaders trying to maintain a sense of control and order with normal Passover festivities. A run of the mill rogue prisoner with a long rap sheet who has few redeeming qualities is suddenly the crowd favorite, while the Messiah who came riding in into town triumphally is knocked off his pedestal spectacularly. Do you remember about ten years ago when Martha Stewart was charged with insider trading and sentenced to jail for 2-3 years? I remember during her trial thinking that I hoped she was sentenced and sent to jail, that she was not above anyone else, but then I wondered later if my desire to see her convicted was really due to my overwhelming sense of justice or because I was like one of the people in this crowd. I saw her with her line of kitchen and home décor, her cooking show, her many books that my wife had acquired, and I was ready to see Martha brought low, I was ready to see her knocked down a few rungs on the ladder, I was ready to see her publicly humiliated. I am telling you this whole scene is one big hot mess; spectacular and disordered, with an overwhelming sense of peculiar fascination.

This Palm Sunday and Passion pattern is not just a once a year curiosity though. It is constantly the way Jesus takes up residency and makes room for himself in our lives. We herald him and go wild as he gets near, we sing and shout and let it all out as he passes by, but already we sense that he is not the king we expected. As the common donkey he is riding on comes into focus and we see no jewels or sequins, no army or political party lining up behind him; and yet strangely, as he begins to shatter our expectations of a Messiah, he begins to shatter and transform our expectations of ourselves and what we want for our lives and who we believe we are called to be. We don't just find the hot mess inside this story, we find it outside, in us, and the more deeply this Savior parades into our lives, the more deeply we see just what a hot mess we are, spectacularly unsuccessful and disordered. And yet this disorderly and disturbing figure parading to his own death is also the very one in whom we will not just be disturbed but made also whole, the very one in who goes from parade to cross will not just confront us but comfort us, the very one who enters our lives and finds them in a mess, will not just leave us to wallow in us, but will stand with us and guide us to find our true purpose and in whose company our lives will be satisfied

Strangely the one figure who does not act all that disorderly or out of control throughout this whole episode is Jesus. He answers Pilate's questions with his own questions, he does not try to instigate a riot when he is arrested on trumped up charges nor does he voice his righteous indignation when a hot mess of a prisoner is released instead of him. Instead of expressing dismay, he seems to suggest that all is going according to plan.

At any rate, all this talk of messes led me back to Christmas. From the events of passion week, the pageantry and nativity scenes and Christmas cookies and twinkling lights seem a distant memory and a far cry from being handed over for crucifixion. But maybe not. In a reflection on Christmas, fellow Presbyterian minister Matt Brown in his book *Parish* reminds us that our Christmas nativities "are always so sanitized, somber, and elegant, (even when) God's advent on earth was anything but sophisticated and chic. However," he writes, "as hard as we try to airbrush the nativity and Photoshop our [own] lives, the original nativity unapologetically proclaims that Christ appears not where we wish our lives could be, but where we are."[36] It is just that he does not leave us there, but asks us to leave behind the things that need to be left behind and follow him in a way of life that will ask that we live as the people he is willing to be handed over and crucified for. Brown reminds us that the original nativity declares very clearly that Christ appears in the midst of the "messiness, embarrassment, and unpolished days of our lives," but he does not come to inspect whether our lives are in order; he knows that they are mess, yet "Jesus jumps right in to help us shovel our way out...out of the dark corners into which we back ourselves...out of the cracked porcelain of our relationships...out of our unwillingness to forgive or be forgiven...out of our inability to see our true gifts and offer them to others..."[37]

He does not just stop entering our messes once he enters this world though. He walks all the way to the cross doing so, parading into our lives and messes, "not in the airbrushed portraits [and social media platforms] of our lives that we want everyone to see," but he walks into the "pain, insecurity, clutter, doubts, splintered images, broken family portraits and do-overs of our real lives."[38] Brown reminds us that Christ does his best work amidst the mess even as he walks into the biggest hot mess of all, taking our place

---

[36] Matt Brown, *Parish* (Resource Publications, Eugene, OR, 2014), 141.

[37] Matt Brown, *Parish*, 142.

[38] Matt Brown, *Parish*, 142.

and rendering our lives more beautiful, meaningful, and significant than we ever thought possible. We are more than unaffected bystanders or a collection of hot messes, but we get caught up in Christ's life and like Barabbas, though we do not deserve it, we are released, we are freed by Christ's life, so that in his service and company, we too may offer our contribution to the world. Amen.

Meanwhile...
I Thessalonians 5:1-18

Now concerning the times and the seasons, brothers and sisters, you do not need to have anything written to you. For you yourselves know very well that the day of the Lord will come like a thief in the night. When they say, "There is peace and security," then sudden destruction will come upon them, as labor pains come upon a pregnant woman, and there will be no escape! But you, beloved, are not in darkness, for that day to surprise you like a thief; for you are all children of light and children of the day; we are not of the night or of darkness. So then let us not fall asleep as others do but let us keep awake and be sober; for those who sleep sleep at night, and those who are drunk get drunk at night. But since we belong to the day, let us be sober, and put on the breastplate of faith and love, and for a helmet the hope of salvation. For God has destined us not for wrath but for obtaining salvation through our Lord Jesus Christ, who died for us, so that whether we are awake or asleep we may live with him. Therefore encourage one another and build up each other, as indeed you are doing. But we appeal to you, brothers and sisters, to respect those who labor among you, and have charge of you in the Lord and admonish you; esteem them very highly in love because of their work. Be at peace among yourselves. And we urge you, beloved, to admonish the idlers, encourage the faint hearted, help the weak, be patient with all of them. See that none of you repays evil for evil, but always seek to do good to one another and to all. Rejoice always, pray without ceasing, give thanks in all circumstances; for this is the will of God in Christ Jesus for you.

When will Christ return? How shall we prepare? And what shall we do? I have no idea if these exact questions were posed to the apostle Paul by the Thessalonians, but our passage certainly seems to be trying to answer questions like these. It's easy to get caught up in the weeds and get myopic isn't it? Who is sitting where at Thanksgiving dinner or resurrecting this or that grudge or worrying over Christmas lists or other end of year anxieties or Uncle Eddie and Aunt Katherine and the kids showing up for longer than expected. We all think we are creatures of control and independence, but we are often so easily overcome and undone by very small and harmless molehills.

As we have heard, the chief anxieties for the Thessalonians were centered around two things: The Day of the Lord, the return of Christ, Judgment Day, and what they should be doing as they waited and anticipated that return. Paul's answer is not exactly the most pastoral and comforting and reassuring is it? In fact, he twice refers to criminal behavior and crime to illustrate his points. 'The day of the Lord will come like a thief in the night,' (v.2) and again in verse four, 'that day (will) surprise you like a thief.' It's like Paul is using a creepy Halloween scary story as an illustration here…'you know how someone breaks into your home and sneaks around while you are comfortably asleep in your beds? That's what the return of Christ will be like.' Oh great. Not exactly a story you want to gather around the hearth and contemplate with your cocoa like the 'Night Before Christmas.'

So for at least the initial verses of our lesson, the day of the Lord Paul is depicting, would not, at least for me, do much to calm my troubled soul but instead would amp up my anxiety even more. 'Oh my, so I cannot plan, there is no way to know, Christ's return and fulfillment are going to be a complete surprise.' There is nothing I can do about it. It is beyond my control and ability to discern. But it is at this exact moment that our passage pivots in a completely different direction. 'Oh wait, it is beyond my control and ability to plan.' Those are not words that should fill us with anxiety at all, but should give us great comfort and joy. 'It is beyond my control and ability. There is nothing I can do about it.'

And so, Paul informs us, while we await the day of the Lord, while we anticipate Christ's fulfillment, there is a certain life we have been called to live in this time between the times. It cannot be done alone. It requires a community; a body of Christ. And there are certain expectations for how we are to live and treat each other. And Paul launches into a beautiful description of what it means to live in this 'meanwhile' between Christ's resurrection and Christ's return, but before he does, in verse 9, he makes perhaps the most central and profound statement in our scripture passage and maybe in all of scripture: 'For God has destined us not for wrath but for obtaining salvation through our Lord Jesus Christ.' God has destined us all, not for destruction, but to belong to God forever. That is our destiny…that is what we have been made for…that is why we are here. Whether we are living or have already died, Paul tells the Thessalonians, life in Christ is what we have been made for, our destiny. Therefore, stop worrying about the day of the Lord or the return of Christ and live lives that 'encourage each other,' and 'build the other up.'

In more naïve days, I used to think that living together as a community that encourages each other and builds each other up was a given, the norm and standard, not anything all that miraculous. But in a world, such a community is far from anything that can be taken for granted. It is a miracle. On our best days, I believe First Presbyterian Church is such a community of faith. Sure we have our flaws and blemishes and warts, but one of the real gifts of this profession, where Seth and Holly and Rhodes and Lynace and our support staff get to sit, is that we get to see glimpses into the particular ways you build each other up and encourage one another as we seek to live as the body of Christ in this place in this time between Christ's resurrection and Christ's return. We encourage each other, and we build each other up, because we see each other as children of God, as those destined not for wrath but for salvation, as those who reflect the grace of our Lord Jesus Christ. And that is a miracle.

But what must it have been like to be part of those early Christians in Thessalonica, anxious about the passing of each day, trying to prepare for the day of the Lord, worried about loved ones dead before Christ's return, and uncertain about what is next? What must it be like to live in such circumstances? I am not sure we could ever know exactly, but perhaps we do have reminders in our own lives from time to time. I have a colleague in ministry who about six months ago was diagnosed with pancreatic cancer. That is not usually a very hopeful diagnosis and certainly not one that any of us want to hear. So over the last many months, he has been coming to terms with this disease, knowing or not knowing how long he will be able to live with this disease. Thankfully, he posts updates from time to time on his Caringbridge site and his most recent post in a way captures some of Paul's sentiments to the Thessalonians as we live our lives before God and anticipate the day of the Lord. I share these excerpts with you now: 'As I have stated before, I spend little time worrying about tomorrow. As Jesus reminded us in the Sermon on the Mount, worrying about tomorrow is a pointless endeavor. You can't worry yourself into a longer life, and you can't worry yourself taller. Worry about tomorrow does nothing to improve tomorrow, and it only ruins today. So this Thanksgiving, my thanks will include: The God who brought me into this world in the first place, and sticks with me. My wife and best friend and family who love me unconditionally. Good friends who know that sometimes I feel like talking about cancer and sometimes I don't. A church community and all who uphold us in prayer and love. Times of worship that lift our hearts and spirits. Doctors and nurses with their generous gifts of time and expertise. The mail carrier, who regularly delivers heartfelt and hopeful cards and letters from far and wide. Others who have been diagnosed with similar illnesses and the opportunity to support each other. A warm and loving home, full of love and peace. Books that carry my mind to all kinds of exciting places. Quiet mornings and good coffee. A life that's already amazingly long; and the gift of each day.'

It is true that we do not know the day or the hour...and that the return of Christ will come as a surprise to us all. But meanwhile...meanwhile, we can be confident that none of us, not one of us, has been destined for wrath, but that God has destined each of us for salvation through Jesus Christ and in this time we have while we wait, we encourage each other and build each other up, we return no one evil for evil, but seek to do good to one another and to all. We rejoice always, we pray without ceasing, we give thanks in all circumstances.

This is a way of life that demands every ounce of our being, full of expectations that will be challenging and difficult for us, even on our best days, but especially those days when we find ourselves in the weeds of life. But God does not ask us to do this by ourselves, but together in a giving and forgiving community of faith that encourages us and builds us up. And such a life is not only for us, or for our own good, but a gift we give each to each other, and it is a gift we give to our world in this 'meanwhile' until Christ's kingdom comes.

Who's Counting?
Matthew 18:21-35

Then Peter came and said to him, 'Lord, if another member of the church sins against me, how often should I forgive? As many as seven times?' Jesus said to him, 'Not seven times, but, I tell you, seventy-seven times. For this reason the kingdom of heaven may be compared to a king who wished to settle accounts with his slaves. When he began the reckoning, one who owed him ten thousand talents was brought to him; and, as he could not pay, his lord ordered him to be sold, together with his wife and children and all his possessions, and payment to be made. So the slave fell on his knees before him, saying, "Have patience with me, and I will pay you everything." And out of pity for him, the lord of that slave released him and forgave him the debt. But that same slave, as he went out, came upon one of his fellow-slaves who owed him a hundred denarii; and seizing him by the throat, he said, "Pay what you owe." Then his fellow-slave fell down and pleaded with him, "Have patience with me, and I will pay you." But he refused; then he went and threw him into prison until he should pay the debt. When his fellow-slaves saw what had happened, they were greatly distressed, and they went and reported to their lord all that had taken place. Then his lord summoned him and said to him, "You wicked slave! I forgave you all that debt because you pleaded with me. Should you not have had mercy on your fellow-slave, as I had mercy on you?" And in anger his lord handed him over to be tortured until he should pay his entire debt. So my heavenly Father will also do to every one of you, if you do not forgive your brother or sister from your heart.'

In the Meantime

I always associate particular smells with this time of year. To this day I can walk across a freshly cut lawn or field and immediately get a touch of nausea with memories of practices long ago and having to run at the end of a long hot practice in the later summer heat. Having played a sport that was half religion and half athletic contest throughout the small town high schools of Texas, I find that particular memories flood back to me this time of year. In particular, I remember standing on a freshly mowed practice field and staring at a sideline full of parents (mainly dads) who were able to cut their day short to oversee each of our practices. I remember looking over one day and giving thanks that my own parents were not there…for a number of reasons…but one of which was that I was glad they had more productive ways to spend their time than managing and overseeing all my practices.

Recently I found myself standing on a sideline full of parents (mainly dads) overseeing practice. Ironic, I know. Thankfully, we were not trying to prescribe plays for the coach to run or play armchair quarterback but were instead (partly I think because of the smells), we were admiring the field and the grass and remembering about our first days of learning to mow the lawn and do yardwork. One of the parents expressed his delight that his child could now start taking over 'yardwork duties,' and how much he looked forward to this transition taking place. I listened silently and intently, if somewhat gloomily. Not because I wish for my children to lay around captive to a screen and not learning to help with the mowing and weed-eating and other chores around our home, but because I enjoy mowing the lawn and doing yardwork and psychologically do not think I am ready to give it up. A lot of the work of ministry, a lot of the work of the church, a lot of the work we all engage in is often hidden, intangible, abstract, and invisible…that does not make it less real or unimportant, but it does make it hard to visualize or see or quantify or easy to produce concrete results. Not so with the yard. One can immediately see the results. One can immediately tell the difference between a freshly mowed yard and an unwieldy one. I like to mow the yard...because I can point to the completion of a job and see the difference. I can finish a project, feel a sense of accomplishment, and move on. But the life of discipleship and the daily opportunity that unfolds before us each day to follow Jesus Christ is not completed so easily, so neatly, so visibly, so evidently. We are never complete...until the return of Christ and the fulfillment of his kingdom.

Awhile back I used to have a picture of C.S. Lewis, the great lay Christian writer and thinker of the mid-20th century, sitting in an easy chair smoking a cigar with the following quotation ascribed to him: 'I didn't go to religion to make my happy. I always knew a bottle of Port would do that. If you want a religion to make you feel comfortable, I certainly don't recommend Christianity.' Perhaps we could amend his statement to add that I didn't go to religion for the successful completion of every project. If we want a religion to be like mowing the lawn with a problem to be solved or a project to be completed or a life full of visible tangible benefits daily, then I certainly don't recommend Christianity either.

In our scripture lesson today, Peter treats forgiveness like mowing the lawn. How many times do I need to do this to successfully complete the project? What must I do to gain mastery over this subject matter? Or as we hear from the servant in this parable, what strategy can I adopt to get me out of this enormous debt that is impossible to payback, so I can continue with my life of calculating and counting. In the words of commentator Robert Capon, the servant's 'first thought on being released was not how to die to his old life and market himself a new one...Rather it was to go on with all his bookkeeping as before.'[39] Who's counting? Well the servant is...the same one who has been forgiven an unheard-of debt is still counting. He summarizes most of my pre-college approach to education and learning: what is the least amount I can do and still get credit?

In contrast to the servant, at the beginning of our passage, Peter puts forward a very generous offer. The Torah did not require such lavish mercy or extensive multiplicities of forgiveness. And the number seven is a very biblical number, representing completeness, fulfillment, mission accomplished. Seven means our work is done. It's a number we can attain and count until our work is done, checking off that to-do list, weeding and edging and mowing until the whole yard of forgiveness is complete and we can move on to other things. But again, Robert Capon reminds us that 'none of our debts, none of our sins, none of our trespasses, none of our errors,' not even if they number seventy-times seven, 'will ever be an obstacle to the grace that raises the dead.' So, it is not so much about counting as it is losing ourselves in the practice of forgiving. Capon adds that if we prefer to keep count or see discipleship as a project we are tasked to complete or if we insist on 'binding others' debts upon them in the name of our own right to life,' then we endanger ourselves of letting God's grace slip through our fingers, we refuse to let God's grace have its way with us or affect us, and we might just risk missing the joy such grace creates in us.[40] That's the problem with counting...we think the Christian life is about completing a problem or accomplishing a project rather than a way of living that will challenge us more deeply than we want to be challenged, ask more of us than we think we can give, and confront us with practices that will not be completed short of Christ's

---

[39] Robert Capon, *Kingdom, Grace, and Judgment*, 198.

[40] Robert Capon, *Kingdom, Grace, and Judgment*, 199.

return. As Lutheran theologian Robert Jenson puts it: 'short of the end, the believer never advances beyond his or her baptism, but instead falls behind it and must catch up to it.'[41] We must catch up to our baptism...the person who dies to sin and is raised to life in Christ...we are on the path of discipleship trying to catch up to that person even as we try to catch up to it seventy-times seven times. It's hard to keep count once we begin to realize that keeping count of sins, forgiveness, or achievements is not what the Christian life was ever supposed to be about.

Several years ago I had the opportunity to pursue doctoral studies and complete a dissertation and I remember feeling proud of the accomplishment. And it was not an easy exercise and required not only a lot of blood, sweat, and tears from me, but also from my family. I remember seeing one of my seminary professors after I completed my dissertation, published it in book form, and was feeling pretty special as I approached him. After congratulating me on my accomplishment and offering some praise, he said, but I do have one question for you. 'What next?' What are your working on next? Where are you going to focus your work now? At the time, I was miffed and a bit stunned that I was not being allowed to revel a little longer in the achievement, but he was exactly right. We are constantly moving forward, striving, and challenging ourselves to catch up to our baptism...to become the people we are in Jesus Christ. To paraphrase theologian Karl Barth, God has chosen blessedness and flourishing and thriving for us, and at the same time, God has chosen rejection, damnation, and condemnation for himself.[42] So after receiving such a gift, after being forgiven such an enormous debt, why would anyone want to go back to the old life of rejection and condemnation and kill or be killed? Only those

---

[41] Robert Jenson, *Systematic Theology Vol..2*, 297.

[42] Karl Barth, *Church Dogmatics* II/1, 177.

In the Meantime

who can't stop counting, only those who cannot die to the tit for tat accounting we so easily fall back on to justify our lives.

Robert Capon puts it this way so beautifully: 'in heaven, there are only forgiven sinners. There are no good guys (or gals), no upright, successful types who, by dint of their own integrity, have been accepted into the great country club in the sky.'[43] In heaven, there are those who have lost count and who have learned stop to counting…but Capon reminds us that hell is also populated by forgiven sinners too…Jesus on the cross dies for them too and 'forgives the baseness of even the worst of us, and he never takes back that forgiveness, not even at the bottom of the bottomless pit.' The only difference is that in heaven forgiveness is received and multiplied and everyone has lost track and stopped counting whereas in hell it is rejected by forgiven sinners who do not think they need it or who prefer to rely on their own uprightness or who insist on the 'old life of the bookkeeping world.'[44]

We live in a world that thrives on keeping count…whether it is keeping up with the Jones or keeping count of personal slights or keeping count of all our successes and triumphs. How can we do anything else but count? How can we not keep track? How many times are we to practice forgiveness? Seven times sounds more than enough. But we belong to God who never started counting in the first place, we are loved by a God who willingly suffered the worst of our own counting, we serve a God who frees us from a life reduced to counting and keeping score, seventy-times seven times. But, who's counting?

---

[43] Robert Capon, *Kingdom, Grace, and Judgment*, 199.

[44] Robert Capon, *Kingdom, Grace, and Judgment*, 200.

Tragic Necessity
Habakkuk 2:1-4; Romans 5:1-5

I will stand at my watch post, and station myself on the rampart; I will keep watch to see what he will say to me, and what he will answer concerning my complaint. Then the LORD answered me and said: Write the vision; make it plain on tablets, so that a runner may read it. For there is still a vision for the appointed time; it speaks of the end, and does not lie. If it seems to tarry, wait for it; it will surely come, it will not delay. Look at the proud! Their spirit is not right in them, but the righteous live by their faith.

Therefore, since we are justified by faith, we have peace with God through our Lord Jesus Christ, through whom we have obtained access to this grace in which we stand; and we boast in our hope of sharing the glory of God. And not only that, but we also boast in our sufferings, knowing that suffering produces endurance, and endurance produces character, and character produces hope, and hope does not disappoint us, because God's love has been poured into our hearts through the Holy Spirit that has been given to us.

Imagine, if you will, that you are a common man or woman in medieval Europe living 500 or 600 years ago. Perhaps you are peasant on a feudal fiefdom or you live in a village like Wittenberg or walled city like Edinburgh or a city-state like Geneva and you are a shopkeeper or cobbler or tradesperson. At the center of your village or town or city center is a local parish church or cathedral where you, your neighbors, and most of the townspeople come to worship. The floors of the cathedral are bare field stone and are cold and hard to kneel on for mass. Some people bring wooden stools but most stand or kneel. There are no pews or places to sit in the nave of the church but on the other side of the screen there is the choir where brothers and monks and choristers sit and chant. At the opposite end of the church is the altar where the priest leads the Latin mass facing away from you. Above the den of your neighbors and townspeople it is near impossible to hear what is being said by the priest in the service. When the words are spoken, and the bread is broken or rather when the priest utters the words in the liturgy, 'hoc est corpus meum,' 'this is my body,' a bell rings and the priest lifts the elements high for all to see, and the crowd quiets down in a moment of holy reverence.

The entire service is conducted in Latin, the language of the Roman Empire, the language adopted by the church of Rome in the fourth century, the language that Jerome used to translate the scriptures into what was called the Vulgate Bible because it translated the scriptures into what was then the vulgar tongue, the common language of the people. Your average medieval commoner 500-600 years ago might have known a few Latin phrases and perhaps some prayers and saints, but the words and language of the mass would have been unintelligible for the most part. Latin was the language of law and education and diplomacy, but not the language of the marketplace or the home or the neighbor and friend in the street. And nearly all medieval persons were illiterate. One of the striking features of the cathedral or local parish church was the stained-glass windows, which reached their height in sophistication and beauty in the high middle ages, between 1150 and 1500. While an illiterate society might not be able to read or understand the language of liturgy and religion, they could engage with the gospel stories and the heroes and heroines of scripture, along with the saints of the church, through stained glass. Medieval cathedrals from Notre Dame to Chartres to Salisbury, York, and Canterbury offered beautiful images of gospel stories to an illiterate medieval population through majestic and physical beauty that sought to impart the majestic nature of God's vastness and beauty and our own smallness in comparison. Stories or figures not depicted in stained glass were rarely known. In the medieval world, unless you were pursuing a university education, further investigation and reading was rare if not impossible. There was no hearing a sermon and wanting to read more. Books were rare commodities and libraries were only kept by the wealthy and well connected. The introduction of the printing press in the middle of the 15th century allowed for printed materials to be produced in mass quantity, cheaply, and also demanded that material be printed in a language familiar to the local populace.

Just like reading, scripture translation, and engagement with written text, congregational singing was a rarity in the local medieval parish or the cathedral church. Yes, there might be Gregorian chants led by monks or brothers from a local priory; cathedral churches might have choristers or a boys choir, but the idea that every person who entered the church had a vocation that could serve God, a mind to seek God's wisdom, and a voice to sing God's praises in the act of communal worship, would have been revolutionary and rare prior to the Reformation. One would not think of singing hymns like 'Now Thank We All our God' around the family hearth or reading Psalm 100 in English as subversive activity. Yet, author Marilynne Robinson reminds us that William Tyndale's translation of the New Testament into the English language (80% of which remained exactly as it was translated about 90 years later in the King James Bible), through such activity 'the Bible may be fairly said to have entered English as a subversive document.'[45] And not only that, but the Reformation was a movement for social justice, not only protesting indulgences that exploited the poor and the devout, but also in the idea that life of faith was meant for everyone whatever

---

[45] Marilynne Robinson, 'Reformation,' in *The Givenness of Things*, 22.

their station and therefore everyone should be able to know and confess and read the scripture of the faith they believed. In William Tyndale's own words: 'I will cause a boy that driveth the plough to know more of Scripture' than a learned scholar or priest.[46] This same impulse led John Knox to seek to establish a school in every parish in Scotland so that boys and girls (no matter their social class, standing, or gender), could learn to read Holy Scripture. By the end of the eighteenth century, Scotland's literacy rate 'would be higher than any other country,' by 1750 as high as 75% and nearly twice as high as much more prosperous and cultured England to the south. During such time a shocked and maybe appalled English observer visiting Scotland noted that 'in the low country of Scotland...the poorest are, in general, taught to read.'[47] The Reformation was not an elitist movement at all, but an egalitarian one that sought to reach and include and engage the ploughman and the common girl and the poor and the impoverished with the gospel of Jesus Christ expressed in the language they spoke in the market and in the field and in the cobblestone streets. Just as Jesus became fully human, so should the words of scripture, incarnating, reaching, and transforming the lives of the people Jesus himself loved and served.

The Reformation ignited a theological revolution or at least a theological recalibration that placed the emphasis not on what we can do to merit salvation, but on the work of Christ 'through whom we have obtained access to the grace in which we stand.'[48] The Reformation ignited a cultural revolution resetting many European communities and nations' relationship with Rome but also their relationship with their rulers. One of the reasons King

---

[46] Marilynne Robinson, 'Reformation,' in *The Givenness of Things*, 22.

[47] Arthur Herman, *How the Scots Invented the Modern World*, 23.

[48] Romans 5:2.

James authorized a version of the Bible under his name is because he did not like some of the translations whose marginal notes questioned the divine right of kings. The Reformation also ignited a literary revolution and the real flowering of languages like German, French, and English as they got out from under Latin as the language of cultural elite. And the Reformation ignited a social revolution putting scripture in the language and hands of the people, reforming worship in a way that sought to offer people across life's social strata the opportunity to pray, sing praises, and hear the Word of God in a language they could comprehend and respond to themselves as servants of the living God.

But not everything about the Protestant Reformation was good. It was a painful church schism which has ignited painful church schisms ever since including very recently in our own Presbyterian family. As I understand it, there are more than 30,000 denominations or forms of Christianity being practiced and by 2050 there will be 50,000 branches, yet Ephesians declares that there is one Lord, one faith, one baptism, and one God and Father of us all. According to the recently deceased Lutheran theologian Robert Jenson, 'the church is catholic when the living Christ is present,' and therefore people like Luther and Calvin and Bucer and Knox and others were not seeking to start a new 'Protestant' church but to make the one church more catholic so that the living Christ might be more visible.[49] In a recent article on the Reformation, theologian George Hunsinger offered a quotation from Isaac the Syrian a seventh century figure who sounds a lot like Paul in our passage from Romans and who sounds a lot like Martin Luther after 1500 years or so later…listen to what he says: 'We are justified by what is from God and not by what is ours. We inherit heaven by what is from Him and not by what is ours. It is

---

[49] Robert Jenson and Carl Braaten, 'Preface,' *The Catholicity of the Reformation*, viii.

said: 'man is not justified before God by his works; and again: let no one boast in works but in the justice, which is from faith. This justice, then, Paul says is not from works but only from faith, that is in Jesus Christ...One is redeemed by grace and not by works, and by faith one is justified, not by one's way of life.'[50] That was from the 7th century...900 years before the Reformation...so let us rejoice in the faith of Jesus Christ that justifies us, and challenges us and invites us to work for greater visible unity with fellow brothers and sisters in Christ whatever their tradition. Who knows, maybe 100, 200, or another 500 years, the Reformation will have helped us to see all justified by faith, but also more catholic even before Christ's kingdom comes. Amen.

---

[50] George Hunsinger, 'Can the Churches Be Reunited?' *Commonweal* (October 15, 2017), https://www.commonwealmagazine.org/can-churches-be-reunited

Even the Unclean Spirits...
Mark 1:21-28

> *They went to Capernaum; and when the sabbath came, he entered the synagogue and taught. They were astounded at his teaching, for he taught them as one having authority, and not as the scribes. Just then there was in their synagogue a man with an unclean spirit, and he cried out, 'What have you to do with us, Jesus of Nazareth? Have you come to destroy us? I know who you are, the Holy One of God.' But Jesus rebuked him, saying, 'Be silent, and come out of him!' And the unclean spirit, throwing him into convulsions and crying with a loud voice, came out of him. They were all amazed, and they kept on asking one another, 'What is this? A new teaching—with authority! He commands even the unclean spirits, and they obey him.' At once his fame began to spread throughout the surrounding region of Galilee.*

Several generations ago it was the radio jingle. Then came the age of the bumper sticker. Then the soundbite. And now we live in the age of the 140-character tweet or Facebook Meme or Instagram post. So maybe the author of Ecclesiastes is right when he laments/and or states matter of factly that there really is 'nothing new under the sun' (Ecclesiastes 1:9). Before any of these mediums, before the birth of Christ, Julius Caesar was already creating ye olde soundbite more than two thousand years ago when after a quick war in in a Mediterranean province, he summed up the efforts of the Roman Army with three words: 'Veni, Vidi, Vici.' 'I came, I saw, I conquered.' All of these mediums have the same ability to communicate a succinct message in a very suggestive and memorable way without leaving a lot of room for retort or conversation or further discussion. So like it or not, that is the world we swim in, and probably contrary to popular belief, it seems to have always been this way whether communicated on papyrus or a bumper sticker or from someone's twitter handle.

Such brief provocative statements jar us and get our attention and arouse an immediate reaction. And I am sure you wouldn't be surprised to know that some of these bumper sticker maxims and social media memes have the ability to get under my skin and send me into orbit. So against my better judgment, I will share a couple with you. Here goes…this one comes from a bumper sticker I saw several years ago: 'Sitting in a church makes you a Christian as much as sitting in a garage makes you a car.' And the second one I believe was a saying spotted on a Facebook meme: 'Don't go to church, be the church.'

I know what you are thinking and maybe you're right: 'you are a man of the cloth,' 'a staid curmudgeonly minister,' of course you are not going to be in favor of anything, especially some pithy bumper sticker that questions the essential place of the church in our lives. 'You are an insider,' I hear you saying, 'you are a company man…of course you are not going to like those bumper sticker soundbites.' But try, if you will, to put aside my personal bias and deconstruct the central communication of these messages. If the church and Christian community have no role in making us a Christian or if nothing happens while sitting in church, then perhaps there is a lot of truth in these statements. We must concede that going to church 'alone' does not make one a Christian nor does sitting in church alone make us one either, but on the other hand, neither does choosing to do something else or devote our time to something else on Sunday morning. It is pretty near impossible to be the church without going to church or to become a Christian without sitting in the midst of the Christian community. Yes, there are exceptions…. Simeon the Stylite is one who comes to mind who was a Christian ascetic who attained notoriety by living for 37 years on top of a small platform at the top of a pillar in what is now modern-day Syria. And there was Julian of Norwich who lived in a small hut or annex in solitude next to the cathedral in Norwich in England. But they are exceptions and I have always wondered, somewhat voyeuristically, how in the world Simeon the Stylite carried out most of life's basic activities and functions living on top a pillar for thirty-seven years. What does all this have to do with our lesson in the first chapter in Mark? Quite a lot I think.

Mark tells us that Jesus goes to the town of Capernaum and his ministry unfolds. How and where does it begin? In the town square? A Roman amphitheater? Out in the wilderness like John? Among a set of VIPs in a special venue? Mark is very succinct and clear. When the Sabbath came, Jesus went to church. That's right. No big fireworks display or dramatic formal announcement. Jesus just gets out of bed and makes his way to the local synagogue, read: church. You can't be the church without going to church, and this is not some smart alecky bumper sticker response or even some curmudgeonly preacherly admonition, these are straight out of Mark's gospel. Jesus begins on the Sabbath and he begins by going to church. You have probably heard me quote Woody Allen's statement that '80% of life is showing up,' and while I may adjust the percentage even higher, I think Jesus shows us just how true that statement is. Jesus shows up. Jesus gets up. Jesus goes to church. And in so doing, Jesus is the church. As we read further, going to church is not the end of the church for Jesus, but just the beginning, just the opening act, but what Jesus brings about cannot and does not seem to happen without the rather mundane and routine habit of getting up and going to church.

It is in the middle of church, maybe right in the middle of his sermon or right in the middle of a deep discussion with the scribes that another dimension of church unfolds. Maybe even a new dimension. Mark tells us that in the normal order of service in the midst of church, a man with what is described as 'an unclean spirit,' interrupted the regular proceedings and cried out in what can only be described in desperate and urgent terms: 'what have you to do with us, Jesus of Nazareth?' The spirit recognizes the threat Jesus poses and long before Peter recognizes Jesus as the Messiah after much hemming and hawing, the unclean spirit pretty much immediately recognizes who Jesus is and declares him right from the start to be 'the Holy One of God.' This is at the beginning of chapter one of Mark. Just to give you a point of contrast, Peter finally summons up the courage and faith to make this claim in chapter eight...after Jesus has walked on water, fed the five thousand, fed another four thousand, stilled a storm, and cured a variety of ailments. Here in chapter one of Mark, the man with the unclean spirit can immediately see both the threat and the power Jesus poses to the normal order of the day in which human lives are ravaged and controlled by demonic impulses. But here on Jesus' command the spirit flees the person and transforms church from a normal habitual humdrum gathering to a community of transformation and astonishment. Mark describes it best: 'They were all amazed and kept saying to each other, 'He even commands the unclean spirits, and they obey him' (Mark 1:27). Jesus goes to church...but that is not the end of the story...Jesus also transforms the church.

We tend to hear words like 'man with the unclean spirit,' or 'Gerasene Demoniac,' and think in terms of some kind of primitive cultural religious condition or voodoo or some kind of psychotic episode and for all we know maybe all of the above are apt descriptions for what was going on in the life of this human being who cries out to Jesus. But the problem with calling it 'primitive cultural condition,' or 'psychotic episode,' or even 'primitive religious mumbo jumbo' is that all those descriptions help us push such a condition farther away from us. Kind of like the term 'minor surgery.' We only call it 'minor surgery' when it is happening to someone else and we only call it 'demon possession' or an 'unclean spirit' when it is happening to someone else, some one of a kind eccentric in a one of a kind episode, but not anything that could threaten or afflict any of us. And why an unclean spirit? Why is *that* the first thing Jesus sets out to transform in the life of humanity on this long road to the reconciliation and transformation of the world?

Recently I was reading an article about one of my favorite congregations, the Corinthians, and how at the beginning of that letter to a people possessed by all kinds of unclean spirits and messes and baggage, Paul reminds them that the God 'revealed in the crucified Jesus could not be more different' from the 'rock stars of the ancient world.'[51] Author Douglas Campbell reminds us that what Paul describes in the crucified Christ is a God who journeys down deep into the human condition, 'ultimately accepting a shameful death,' a 'reaching God,' 'who values everyone, including the most despised and marginalized.'[52] Especially those with unclean spirits…whether they were lepers or from the wrong side of Samaria or from the wrong social class or condition. Author and novelist Marilynne Robinson puts it this way, even more directly: 'does the word 'stranger,' the word 'alien,' ever have a negative connotation in scripture? No.'[53]

---

[51] Douglas A. Campbell, 'Culture Wars at Corinth,' in *The Christian Century* (January 3, 2018), 29.

[52] Douglas A. Campbell, 'Culture Wars at Corinth,' in *The Christian Century* (January 3, 2018), 29.

[53] Maryilynne Robinson, 'Awakening,' in *The Givenness of Things*, 106.

And that is because as we will confess about God in our creed, that in Jesus Christ, not only are our unclean spirits liberated and fall under his lordship, but Christ has descended into hell. Thus we believe that God has gone the infinite distance away from God and that by descending into hell, God endured and did away once and for all with any state of god forsakenness, emptiness, and nonbeing. So then, whatever trial, hell, or struggle we may be experiencing, God has not only endured and stood in our place in such circumstances, but God has gone the infinite distance away from God, so that there is no place in all creation, even Hell, that is Godless. As we learn from Karl Barth, 'we may choose to live without God, but God never chooses to live without us.' Even in hell. We may have anxieties and unclean spirits in us, but as we learn from the very beginning of Mark, Jesus is not afraid of descending right into them, reaching out to them, liberating us, and transforming our lives. For Jesus, there are no unclean spirits or people after he is done with them. There are no lost causes or unworthy people outside the bounds of his love. No aliens or refugees either…only children of God…fully transformed and fully alive.

Jesus goes to church….and so did we…but that is not the end of the story…. for him or for us. Amen.

Part III: Second Advent

Un-Godlike
I Corinthians 1:18-25

[18] For the message about the cross is foolishness to those who are perishing, but to us who are being saved it is the power of God. [19] For it is written,

"I will destroy the wisdom of the wise,

and the discernment of the discerning I will thwart."

[20] Where is the one who is wise? Where is the scribe? Where is the debater of this age? Has not God made foolish the wisdom of the world? [21] For since, in the wisdom of God, the world did not know God through wisdom, God decided, through the foolishness of our proclamation, to save those who believe. [22] For Jews demand signs and Greeks desire wisdom, [23] but we proclaim Christ crucified, a stumbling block to Jews and foolishness to Gentiles, [24] but to those who are the called, both Jews and Greeks, Christ the power of God and the wisdom of God. [25] For God's foolishness is wiser than human wisdom, and God's weakness is stronger than human strength.

Kate Bowler is in her thirties, teaches at Duke Divinity School, and was recently diagnosed with stage 4 cancer. I am in the midst of reading her account of her struggle to live in a book called *Everything Happens for a Reason: And Other Lies I've Loved*. She is a Canadian who grew up in a Mennonite faith family. Mennonites are direct descendants of the Radical Reformation and while being set apart and sectarian, they have held to their radical beliefs of 'pacifism, simplicity,' and in her words, 'the ability to compliment your neighbor's John Deere Turbo Combine without envy.' Bowler reminds us that while 'Mennonites are best known by their bonnets and horse-drawn buggies,' and their suspicions of modern advances being good for us, 'for the most part,' she reminds us, 'they are plainclothes capitalists like the rest of us.'[54]

Bowler's area of scholarship is what is called the 'prosperity gospel,' a modern phenomenon that what God wants more than anything else, is to shower our lives with blessings, wealth, and to make our lives at ease and comfortable. In short: follow these rules and God will reward you, God will heal you, God will restore you, God will bless you. Bowler began to be interested in this form of religion after it invaded her own Mennonite faith tradition and struck her to her core 'when a number of Mennonites in (her) hometown' starting attending a megachurch and 'began to give money to a pastor who drove a motorcycle onstage.' 'How could Mennonites,' she asked, 'of all people—a tradition once suspicious of the shine of chrome bumpers and the luxury of lace curtains,'[55] now attend a congregation that believes the gospel of Jesus Christ is primarily about self-improvement, human potential, and spiritual achievement, or just amassing as much as possible or at least more than our neighbors and close competition?

These struggles as new and recent as they sound, are not new at all, but have been going on in the life of the Christian community all the way back to the Corinthians who are front and center in our scripture lesson today. In short order, the Corinthians had taken the good news of Christ's death for the sake of the world and turned it into a spiritual pecking order in which the spiritual elite, those who had superior insider knowledge of God were elevated to the highest status in the spiritual pecking order and attained true wisdom. To truly know God, these Corinthians argued, was to attain a special secret wisdom, and that was the way to God. After all, they believed God would never stoop so low as to actually take on a vulnerable human life much less an 'extraordinarily gruesome death,' and so they shifted the focus of

---

[54]Kate Bowler, 'Death, the Prosperity Gospel, and Me,' in *SundayReview New York Times*, February 13, 2016.

[55] Kate Bowler, 'Death, the Prosperity Gospel, and Me,' in *SundayReview New York Times*, February 13, 2016.

the Christian faith from one centered in Christ's death on a cross, to a faith obsessed with attaining 'privileged spiritual knowledge as the way to salvation.'[56] The notion that a deity would secure the salvation of the entire cosmos through a 'degrading, state-sponsored execution,' was so absurd and so un-godlike, that they sought to make their version of Christianity more palatable, less redemptive suffering, less about the cross and the physical suffering of Jesus, which any good Greek knows that God can't suffer, and more on spiritual enlightenment and the quest for moving up the spiritual ladder.

Fleming Rutledge reminds us that in our own day, our own 'stock-in-trade is "positive thinking," with its partner, avoidance—blocking out difficult and painful issues,' and thinking faith is more about getting in touch with our 'inclination to experiment with ever newer and exotic sensations, including 'spiritual ones.'[57] Against this reductionistic approach to religion, 'the Christian gospel places the cross.'[58] And so in Paul's introductory salvo to the Corinthians, Paul reminds them the center of the Christian community will never be defined by a quest for spiritual wisdom and enlightenment but will be found in the proclamation of Christ crucified (v.22), a stumbling block to the spiritually enlightened and foolishness to those who prefer to define their faith in terms of knowledge and wisdom. The cross is pretty much the last place in the world to go looking for God, the last place in the world to think God would appear, and the last place in the world to find the power of God. It should be a failure, a tragedy, a place where good was defeated by evil, a place of injustice and outrage, but according to Paul it is nothing of the kind; instead it is the wisdom of God and 'the best and most wonderful thing God ever did was to die a felon's death, between two robbers.'[59]

---

[56] Fleming Rutledge, *The Crucifixion*, p.70, 46.

[57] Fleming Rutledge, *The Crucifixion*, p.70.

[58] Fleming Rutledge, *The Crucifixion*, p.70.

[59] Philip Rheinlander, *Faith of the Cross*, 81-82, from Fleming Rutledge, *The Crucifixion*, 71.

We all have those long days. Sometimes at the end of a long day there is feeling of weary accomplishment. As I head out of the church and make my way to the car, there is a feeling of tiredness but also a feeling of completion...maybe after a long session meeting or a stimulating bible study or an enriching worship service. I'm tired, but I also feel like something really good and important was accomplished that day...or that might be the emotion even if it is left unspoken. Other times on the walk out to the car, it can also feel a bit more forlorn and flailing. What on earth do I have to show for myself today, Lord? A long list of unanswered emails...a meeting where we have spun our wheels...an inability to get anything accomplished...bad news about somebody's health or somebody's death. We all have those long days too. It affects the mood. It gives us restless sleep. Or it wakes us up suddenly. There is feeling of tiredness, but no accompanying feeling of accomplishment. Just unease...incompleteness...disappointment.

We Presbyterians are not big into crucifixes, but strangely in the chapel of Austin Presbyterian Theological Seminary, there is a crucifix. Even more strangely, it is not in the chancel or up in the front of the chapel for everyone to see, but rather it is hidden in a corner of the transept facing toward the pulpit, where really it cannot be seen by much of the gathered congregation at all unless they are specifically looking for it. It can be seen and it is meant to be seen by the preacher mainly, lurking in their direct line of sight, reminding them that they are not religious virtuosos, but that they are called to proclaim the gospel of one who suffered and died in such a way. The crucifix is not an object of devotion for the congregation as much as it is a strong reminder to the preacher as to our true content and the God who is to be proclaimed.

Many times on that walk to the car at the end of the day, though, I am not by myself. In fact, out of the corner of my eye, also in my direct line of vision, is a school bus, with its engine purring, sitting outside our Christian Education building. As I am heading home, self-satisfied in my accomplishments or hanging my head over my fiascos, I am often confronted and if paying attention, overtaken by that bus sitting there. As it idles, no one is yet on it, but it is warming up and getting ready. The children who ride that bus are still inside the church, our church, inside the Christian Education building. They are participants in the Homeless Education Enrichment Program; and they are homeless children who live in Caddo Parish and who participate in afterschool enrichment activities housed at our church each week. Their lives are in flux and the odds are already stacked against them. Like the crucifix before the preacher, that school bus reminds me that what I have been able to do or what I have failed to do is really very trivial in light of a simple act by a church to welcome and support homeless children in our community. Unbeknownst to them, these children and that bus put my life in perspective and remind me of the God who shows up in the least likely of places, the Lord who becomes a servant, the God who comes to us in what looks like foolishness and debasement and yet turns our world upside down and invades our lives with his disruptive grace. In the midst of our self-satisfied accomplishments and our colossal blunders, this God has a way of taking over the scene, reorienting us, and revealing to us over and over again that the way we find our lives is in giving them away; and by a miracle of grace, we are able to see out of the corner of our eyes, the places where the crucified and risen Lord is at work. Amen.

Outliers
Mark 1:14-20

Now after John was arrested, Jesus came to Galilee, proclaiming the good news of God, and saying, "The time is fulfilled, and the kingdom of God has come near; repent, and believe in the good news." As Jesus passed along the Sea of Galilee, he saw Simon and his brother Andrew casting a net into the sea—for they were fishermen. And Jesus said to them, "Follow me and I will make you fish for people." And immediately they left their nets and followed him. As he went a little farther, he saw James son of Zebedee and his brother John, who were in their boat mending the nets. Immediately he called them; and they left their father Zebedee in the boat with the hired men and followed him.

It is not all that clear to me that what Jesus does here in this passage is necessary or makes a lot of sense. Yes, we need a savior, so God becomes incarnate to restore us and all creation to himself, and that is why Christmas is so important. And yes, we can't live a faithful life and so we need a faithful example not only to show us how to live truly faithfully as human beings, but also to live a life that is pleasing to God in place of all the flawed and fouled up ways human beings have lived life. So, there's that. And as we hear at the beginning of our scripture lesson, there is the divine desire to bring the kingdom of God near and to fulfill God's intention for humanity, and to show us God's true identity in the life of Jesus Christ. That is what happens in our first verse of our scripture lesson…John the Baptist is arrested and continues to exit stage left, and Jesus emerges in Galilee proclaims the good news of God and telling everyone that the moment is upon us, the time is fulfilled, and the kingdom of God is among near and standing before the world in the flesh, gazing upon us face to face. That is all well and good. That is all important to God's vision for humanity and reconciliation of the world. That makes sense. What doesn't make sense is what Jesus does next. As he passes along the sea of Galilee, he sees Peter and Andrew minding their own business, plying their trade, and casting their nets to the sea. And Jesus said to them, "Follow me and I will make you fish for people."

Why do that? He can redeem humanity without doing that. He can bring the kingdom of God up close without doing that. He can live the faithful life without doing that. He can cure diseases, make sick people healthy, give sight to the blind, give hearing to the deaf, he can raise the dead, and preach in parables. So why on earth does he need Peter and Andrew and Holly and Archer and Jesse and Carl and you and me? We are trouble. Our lives are messy. Our abilities are sketchy. We have baggage. That's why we need a Redeemer in the first place. So why on earth would his first act of business be to call us to join him in his work? It makes no sense. He does not need us. He could do it without us. He has seen our resumes. But he passes by the Sea of Galilee and sees those 'happy simple fisherfolk,'[60] and he cannot help himself. He calls them to follow and tells them that from now on, their lives are going to be spent fishing for people.

The last time we had a major snow in Shreveport was during the 2015 Murray lectures, so I hope we have gotten our 2018 snow out of the way already. But one of the things that happened during that snow was that our Murray lecturer, William Willimon, got to spend a little extra time with us. In one of us conversations or talks, he brought up a conversation a group of church leaders and seminary leaders had with some Silicon Valley executives including some

---

[60] William Alexander Percy, 'They Cast Their Nets in Galilee,' in *The Hymnbook*, 355.

Google executives about leading and being a successful organization. At one point one of the Google executives said something that astonished this group of fledging church leaders trying to get ahead or find a new approach or technique that would lead to success. 'Look,' she said, 'we are the ones that should be learning from you. You have found a way to adapt and be innovative and to be around for the last two thousand years. We have had astonishing success, but we are only in our infancy.'

I thought about that statement not long ago upon reading a prominent theological scholar in a recent book worry about the theological threat to the church of the shopping mall. In his book, he shared his belief that the 'local mall is actually one of the most religious sites in town.' He goes on to make the point that while no one at the local shopping mall requires a statement of faith or lists ten things the mall believes, 'the shopping mall is very much interested in what you love,' and capturing your heart or at least some of your treasure. The author continues describing the liturgy of the mall through the architecture of the building, the 'glass atriums at the entrances framed by banners and flags; familiar texts and symbols on the exterior walls help the foreign faithful quickly and easily identify what's inside; and the sprawling layout of the building is anchored by larger pavilions or sanctuaries akin to the vestibules of medieval cathedrals....' He continues that we come to the mall expectant, 'knowing what we need must be there, and that we go to the mall' searching for the experience and 'offering that will provide us fulfillment' which occurs at the altar (cash register) with the priest (cashier) transacting us with the tangible realities of the good life.[61]

---

[61] James K.A. Smith, *You Are What You Love: The Spiritual Power of Habit*, 40-45.

There was probably a time when the shopping mall was a great threat or competitor to the church, but right now I go to the shopping mall not out of some kind of inner spiritual tug-of-war, I go out of civic duty and for fear of Amazon.com taking over the entire world. What was once seen as a great threat to the life and faith of the church, not all that many years ago, is now on the precipice of collapse. I share with you just one title from a recent article from Time magazine, dated July 2017...'Why the Death of the Malls Is About More Than Shopping,' which claims that for more and more Americans, because 'our digital lives are frictionless and ruthlessly efficient, with retail and romance available at a click, shopping 'malls were built for patterns of social interaction that increasingly don't exist,' according to Harvard business professor Leonard Schlesinger.

Let me be clear here. I am not an advocate for or against the shopping mall, but what was still seen as a great threat to the Christian community when this book was published as many years ago as 2016, is now on the verge of extinction. Jesus' seemingly haphazard and irrational decision to call those disciples and people like you and me to the ministry of the church has a remarkable staying power, no matter what the flavor of the month is or what the new hot relevant thing may be. While Jesus did not seem to need to do it and for all we know Jesus might have gotten along better without us, Jesus refuses to carry out his ministry in the world, Jesus refuses to bring about his kingdom, Jesus refuses to live his life without the church, without Peter and Andrew, James and John, you and me.

In his book *Bowling Alone*, sociologist Robert Putnam traced civic groups, garden clubs, bowling leagues, neighborhood community groups, and church communities, and observed that 'for the first two-thirds of the twentieth century a powerful tide drove

Americans into ever deeper engagement in the life of communities, but a few decades ago, silently, without warning, that tide reversed, and we were over taken by a treacherous rip current. Without at first noticing,' he writes, 'we have been pulled apart from one another and from our communities over the last third of the century.'[62] Hyper-individualism and all the benefits of greater independence and personal autonomy have a dark side, which includes greater social isolation and loneliness which psychiatrist Martin Seligman reminds us can best be supported and transformed when one can fall back on family, church, community, and God. 'When we fail to reach some of our personal goals, as we all must, you can turn to these larger institutions for hope,' he writes, 'but in a self standing alone without the buffer of a [community] and larger beliefs, helplessness and failure can all too easily become hopelessness and despair.'[63]

In a way, Jesus' call to discipleship is not just a call to follow him and to reflect his vision and life, but Jesus' call to the disciples, whether they be Peter and Andrew, James or John, Amy or Karen or Anne or Kris, this call is also an attempt to save us from ourselves and to use us and our lives for a larger purpose in the life of our world. As we give thanks for new leaders and those who have answered Christ's call, as we ordain and install them, one thing I hope we see and work for is that this church continues to be a statistical outlier in our world. A church made up of different ideologies and causes and backgrounds united in mission and service to Jesus Christ. A church made up of different ages and generations who sit on the pew together, break bread together, weep and laugh together, and offer our world a witness of the kingdom of God. A church with vibrant worship that does not

---

[62] Robert Putnam, *Bowling Alone*, 27.

[63] Robert Putnam, *Bowling Alone*, 264.

chase after every new thing but is confident that what we are doing here feeds the soul, grabs ahold of the heart, transforms the mind, and makes an impact in the world outside these walls. On some days, I do not really worry about what the larger statistical trends indicate, because I do not think this church, or the God to whom we belong, is captive to such trends. We seek to live in our world as an aberration, as statistical outliers, just as Peter and Andrew did on the bank of the Sea of Galilee. Jesus did not have to call us; he could have done it all by himself. But he refuses to do it without us. So let us continue to thrive and be a community of faith, hope, and love, a refuge from social isolation, a place full of interesting happenings and interesting people, and most of all, an interesting God.

We are statistical outliers. We're not supposed to be here. Jesus could have done it all by himself. Yet here we are. And Jesus said to them, 'Follow me and I will make you fish for people.' Amen.

Now Thank We All Our God
Matthew 21:33-46

"Listen to another parable. There was a landowner who planted a vineyard, put a fence around it, dug a wine press in it, and built a watchtower. Then he leased it to tenants and went to another country. When the harvest time had come, he sent his slaves to the tenants to collect his produce. But the tenants seized his slaves and beat one, killed another, and stoned another. Again he sent other slaves, more than the first; and they treated them in the same way. Finally he sent his son to them, saying, 'They will respect my son.' But when the tenants saw the son, they said to themselves, 'This is the heir; come, let us kill him and get his inheritance.' So they seized him, threw him out of the vineyard, and killed him. Now when the owner of the vineyard comes, what will he do to those tenants?" They said to him, "He will put those wretches to a miserable death and lease the vineyard to other tenants who will give him the produce at the harvest time."

Jesus said to them, "Have you never read in the scriptures:

'The stone that the builders rejected
  has become the cornerstone;
this was the Lord's doing,
  and it is amazing in our eyes'?

Therefore, I tell you, the kingdom of God will be taken away from you and given to a people that produces the fruits of the kingdom. The one who falls on this stone will be broken to pieces; and it will crush anyone on whom it falls."

When the chief priests and the Pharisees heard his parables, they realized that he was speaking about them. They wanted to arrest him, but they feared the crowds, because they regarded him as a prophet.

What a crummy story. This landowner builds a vineyard and mysteriously leaves and hands over everything to the tenants. The cat goes away, and the mice play and suddenly our story turns into a scene from *Lord of the Flies* as the landowner sends servants to harvest the vineyard and they end up beaten, violently returned to sender and even killed. One after another messenger is killed until the landowner has to send a larger delegation to collect the fruit of the vineyard from the tenants. The larger party is treated as shabbily and violently as the others and are beaten and killed until they are driven away. Finally, enough is enough and the landowner sends his own son…instead of fear or respect or thinking okay enough is enough, the tenants see the opportunity and take the landowner's son out, so they acquire the vineyard to do with as they wish rather than cultivate it for the landowner. So the son arrives and they kill him too. End of story. It's like a scene from the 'Godfather.' A crummy story, a sordid story, a violent story that ends with Jesus' admonition and judgment that the 'kingdom of God will be taken away' from such people and given to a people that 'produce the fruits of the kingdom.'

This is a passage full of violence, full of people repeatedly exhibiting the most destructive behavior, servants who have seized the opportunity to exercise the sovereignty of self over against the sovereignty of their Lord. At the beginning of last week, I actually wondered and worried if such a passage might have much to say to our world now, but that was before the carnage of Las Vegas and the now largest mass shooting in our nation's history…and I hate even saying that because such references just become benchmarks for others to strive for. Our scripture passage is full of cyclical destructiveness, demented violence, and troubled and ungrateful lives, and so is our world. I spent most of the past week with a gathering of minister colleagues reading through John Calvin's 1541 edition of the *Institutes of Christian Religion*. This is a group of colleagues who gather together to read theology because we believe it shapes ministry in significant ways and shapes us too for our calling. But I know you've also got to be thinking that such an endeavor sounds a bit esoteric, arcane, and out of touch, if not goofy. Who in their right mind would choose to do that? But one of the many insights gleaned from the week was that John Calvin saw that the chief sin of humanity, the chief sin that infects our hearts and lives, our chief sin of all sins that leads to all the others is that of ingratitude. Not pride. Not selfishness. Not hubris. Not greed. Not gluttony or anger or lust or covetousness, but ingratitude. Our ingratitude, at least in Calvin's view, leads to all our other destructive behaviors. After all, gratitude is an awareness that we are creatures of God and that we belong to God and that we are part of something bigger than ourselves in this world, and that leads to a life of gratefulness and praise and awe. Ingratitude keeps us from ever fully becoming human, ever seeing our neighbor before us as gift...instead people become projects or problems to be solved or worse, lives to be shot at indiscriminately and in cold blood. Maybe the greatest threat we as a society, we as a country face is a kind of homegrown domestic terrorism that is not fueled by any particular religion or beliefs at all but is the product of a nihilistic ingratitude that believes in nothing and has no regard for human life. Could all the problems of our world, of our lives, all the tragedies and inexplicable violence that are now part of our regular occurrence and that have sadly become the 'new normal,' could all of this be explained by hearts turned in upon themselves and an inability to live life with any kind of gratitude?

I don't know that evil can be explained or that we can easily reduce evil and darkness to one word or that we can or even should try to explain such destructive and violent acts in any rational way, but I do think (or at least I hope) that such despicable acts can only be carried out by people who can no longer see mothers and fathers and children and neighbors but only indiscriminate two-dimensional targets on a practice range. How could one see another human life, a neighbor, a mother, a child of God, and still take that life, unless completely blinded by an ungrateful inward nihilism with no regard for human life?

We see it in the actions of the wicked tenants in this passage and we see in the violent actions of a wicked and malicious gunmen in Las Vegas, in both cases revealing to us the worst in ourselves and the worst in humanity that takes God's gifts and casts them aside or maybe even worse, ungratefully possesses God's gifts as our own to do with as we please. We often tend to define freedom as doing whatever we please, but as we see in the spiral of violence and destructiveness of the tenants, doing as we please is not liberating at all, but leads to self-imprisonment, it de-humanizes us and our neighbor, and makes us possessive and violent and ungrateful. Preserving ourselves and the false freedom of doing whatever we please unleashes greater destruction. Freedom to do as we please is anything but liberating; what liberates us is living a life of gratitude, a life given over to loving God and loving neighbor, a life of generosity and sharing our resources with others and for the betterment of the world around us.

The landowner in this scripture lesson does act strangely. He does not act like a boss or micro-manager. He gives this beautiful gift to these tenants, gets the vineyard going, digs the wine press and a tower, and then mysteriously leaves for another country and entrusts them with the run of the place. Rather than caring for the gift they have been given and trying to produce fruit for the landowner, the tenants spend all their time scheming to take possessions of the land themselves and killing all those sent by the landowner who threaten them or threaten to take what they think is rightfully theirs. What is interesting is that the landowner relentlessly and faithfully sends servants to collect the produce of this land. He continues to send them faithfully, over and over again, even his own son, so that this people will receive life as a gift and not something to be possessed and demarcated, to kill or be killed over. Over and over again he keeps sending people into their lives so that they will produce the fruits of his kingdom.

About 400 years ago, a German musician and church deacon Martin Rinkart, lived in the small city of Eilenburg during the 30 Years War, which took place for the most part in Germany, and which was a sad outcome of the Reformation and Counter-Reformation and wars over property and rights and Catholic and Protestant identity. In addition to the war, the plague also made a pass through Germany and the European continent so that due to war or plague, one of every three people died during this Thirty Years War. Rinkart's Eilenburg was a microcosm of this and as an archdeacon and one of the last surviving ministers in the city, Rinkart helped house refugees to the city at great personal expense and was officiating as many as fifty funerals a day and more than a thousand funerals a year. It was in the midst of such violence, death, despair, and seeing humanity at its worst, that Rinkart also composed a prayer to be sung around the table at family devotions. This prayer later became the hymn, 'Now Thank We All our God,' and thanks God with heart and hand and voices, a God who does wondrous things in this world and in our lives, a God who blesses us with countless gifts of love, and still is ours today.' This prayer and hymn did not come out of a time when one's life was on top of the world and all was calm in the world, but it came out of the depths of life, out of the depths of human struggle, out of the depths of brutality and death, and yet it is not a funeral dirge, nor does it signal a note of despair, but comes from a life of gratitude lived before God.

Are we living in such desperate and frightening times? If we are, I hope, and I believe the church's witness can often shine the brightest when it is darkest, and that a life of gratitude might just be what we have to offer our world that will turn swords to plowshares and an ungrateful nihilism into the fruits of God's kingdom. Amen.

Both And...
Matthew 25:31-46

"When the Son of Man comes in his glory, and all the angels with him, then he will sit on the throne of his glory. All the nations will be gathered before him, and he will separate people one from another as a shepherd separates the sheep from the goats, and he will put the sheep at his right hand and the goats at the left. Then the king will say to those at his right hand, 'Come, you that are blessed by my Father, inherit the kingdom prepared for you from the foundation of the world; for I was hungry and you gave me food, I was thirsty and you gave me something to drink, I was a stranger and you welcomed me, I was naked and you gave me clothing, I was sick and you took care of me, I was in prison and you visited me.' Then the righteous will answer him, 'Lord, when was it that we saw you hungry and gave you food, or thirsty and gave you something to drink? And when was it that we saw you a stranger and welcomed you, or naked and gave you clothing? And when was it that we saw you sick or in prison and visited you?' And the king will answer them, 'Truly I tell you, just as you did it to one of the least of these who are members of my family, you did it to me.' Then he will say to those at his left hand, 'You that are accursed, depart from me into the eternal fire prepared for the devil and his angels; for I was hungry and you gave me no food, I was thirsty and you gave me nothing to drink, I was a stranger and you did not welcome me, naked and you did not give me clothing, sick and in prison and you did not visit me.' Then they also will answer, 'Lord, when was it that we saw you hungry or thirsty or a stranger or naked or sick or in prison, and did not take care of you?' Then he will answer them, 'Truly I tell you, just as you did not do it to one of the least of these, you did not do it to me.' And

these will go away into eternal punishment, but the righteous into eternal life."

Finally, a parable I can relate to. Finally, a lesson I can understand and figure out. There is black and there is white. There is good and there is bad. Good little sheep are rewarded, and wicked little goats are punished. Good deeds on the one hand, no deeds on the other. A straightforward moral. Finally, at the Last Judgment, we see, in commentator Robert Capon's words, we see Jesus taking off 'the velvet glove of grace and putting on the brass knuckles.'[64]

But not so fast. As Capon himself reminds us, Jesus spends a lot of time throughout the witness of scripture reminding us that grace does not discriminate between good and bad and even works on some pretty contemptible characters like a prodigal son who is far from putting his life back together when he is welcomed home and 'eleventh-hour laborers' who could not possibly have earned their pay in such a brief time.[65] So why is it that this parable about sheep and goats seems so clearly to depict goodness as a prerequisite for salvation and badness as a prerequisite for condemnation? Here we were led to believe and trust in God's radical grace only to get to the Last Judgment and find out it's all about keeping score and our moral record after all? It's all back to worrying after all whether we have been counted as a good sheep or bad goat?

But as you might have guessed by now, I am not so sure about such a straightforward reading of this parable. For starters, this Good Shepherd is a shepherd of both the sheep and the goats, and throughout scripture Jesus does not act as if 'badness is an obstacle to his kingdom,' nor does he make 'goodness one of its entrance

---

[64] Robert Capon, *Parables of the Kingdom, Grace, and Judgment*, 509.
[65] Robert Capon, *Parables of the Kingdom, Grace, and Judgment*, 508.

requirements,' therefore prodigals and tax collectors and prostitutes and Samaritans are accepted and welcomed and bearers of the gospel, whereas much more upstanding and respectable characters clumsily flail and fail and miss out on the gospel of grace.[66]

Ralph Wood, who teaches religion and literature at Baylor University, once wrote that the 'aim of the gospel is not to get us into Heaven so much as to get Heaven into us, and thus to get the Hell out of us.'[67] The point of life is not about trying to tick boxes that will guarantee us entry into heaven as it is trying to get heaven into us right now. Perhaps a sifting does occur at the Final Judgment, but that rather than being a Manichean-black-and-white-good-and-evil, us-and-them type of outward separation, the sifting that occurs takes our whole life and beyond for God to complete us and get the Heaven into us and the hell out of us, to get the sheep into us and the goat out of us. Think about what this king says at the end of the parable. Robert Capon reminds us that he does not say that 'the sheep have compiled a splendid moral record,' but that they sought to see the face of the King in the least likely of people and places. They believed they could see the presence of the King in even the most implausible and questionable candidates. It is not their deeds that gain them a reward but their belief in a deity who loves a world full of such people. It is the way they have been able to use the gift they have been given to see the life of this King unfolding in the lives of the poor, the sick, the hungry, and the thirsty. To paraphrase Martin Luther: no one 'can know (for certain) or feel he (or she) is saved; one can only believe it.'[68] One can only trust it and trust in a God

---

[66] Robert Capon, *Parables of the Kingdom, Grace, and Judgment*, 507.

[67] Ralph Wood, 'A Call for a Latter-Day Reformation of the Church,' sermon preached at First Baptist Church, Hendersonville, North Carolina, January 1997, 2.

[68] From Robert Capon, *Parables of the Kingdom, Grace, and Judgment*, 511.

who is Lord of both the sheep and the goats and who continually gives his life in order to get Heaven into us and hell out of us.

A small group of us spent the past four weeks reading through Martin Luther's 95 Theses to coincide with the 500th anniversary of the Reformation and also to say we had accomplished something, to say we had read all 95 theses together. The very first thesis statements sets the tone, not only for Luther's emphasis, but I think for our passage today. Luther expresses it this way: 'When our Lord and Master Jesus Christ said, 'Repent,' he willed the entire life of believers to be one of repentance.' In other words, all of life is about getting heaven into us and hell out of us, and it does not ever end until God makes all things new and fulfills God's purposes for us. It would be easier to see the world as 100% sheep or 100% goats, but we all have hooves and horns and wool with all the characteristics of both creatures. I try not to be a dispenser of pithy quotations, but I saw one recently that said it is not the 'size of the storms in our life that matters, but the size of the God.' And I think a similar expression is formed by this passage. It is this God of both the sheep and the goats that ultimately prevails, and we can gladly place our trust in his grace and judgment rather than our own attempts to determine who the occupants of the new Jerusalem might be. We can rest assured that the God of the Last Judgement is the same God who forgives sinners, welcomes outcasts, heals the sick, and raises the dead. It is the God, who like the prodigal son, goes to a foreign and far country, to bring us back home. A God who is more interested in getting heaven into us, then getting us into heaven, a God, who sees the sheep in us even when we are lost in a herd of goats…a God who refuses to be finished with both the sheep and the goats until we all become what he intended all along…in this life…and in the life to come. Amen.

Known by the Company You Keep
Matthew 21:23-32

When he entered the temple, the chief priests and the elders of the people came to him as he was teaching, and said, "By what authority are you doing these things, and who gave you this authority?" Jesus said to them, "I will also ask you one question; if you tell me the answer, then I will also tell you by what authority I do these things. Did the baptism of John come from heaven, or was it of human origin?" And they argued with one another, "If we say, 'From heaven,' he will say to us, 'Why then did you not believe him?' But if we say, 'Of human origin,' we are afraid of the crowd; for all regard John as a prophet." So they answered Jesus, "We do not know." And he said to them, "Neither will I tell you by what authority I am doing these things. "What do you think? A man had two sons; he went to the first and said, 'Son, go and work in the vineyard today.' He answered, 'I will not'; but later he changed his mind and went. The father went to the second and said the same; and he answered, 'I go, sir'; but he did not go. Which of the two did the will of his father?" They said, "The first." Jesus said to them, "Truly I tell you, the tax collectors and the prostitutes are going into the kingdom of God ahead of you. For John came to you in the way of righteousness and you did not believe him, but the tax collectors and the prostitutes believed him; and even after you saw it, you did not change your minds and believe him.

How do you measure success? Or for all of us, how do we become successful Christians? What does that look like? The Lutheran and later Roman Catholic priest and writer Richard John Neuhaus posted a quotation on the wall of his study from Ralph Waldo Emerson about success. 'How do you measure success? To laugh often and much; to win the respect of intelligent people and the affection of children; to earn the appreciation of honest critics and endure the betrayal of false friends; to appreciate beauty; to find the best in others; to leave the world a bit better, whether by a healthy child, a redeemed social condition, or a job well done; to know even one other life has breathed because you lived—this is to have succeeded.'[69] Such a description is very thoughtful and humane and worthy rather than the definitions of financial, material, and spiritual security that often become our defacto ways of defining what it means to be successful or comfortable or happy in our world. Neuhaus was moved enough by the statement that he put it on his wall as a reminder, and yet he also reminds us that for Christians, we are radically liberated by a grace beyond all our criteria of effectiveness or success. We cannot and do not have to legitimate our lives or the church's life in any respectable way...or to borrow from Neuhaus' beautiful prose: 'we do not need to sniff around the secular criterion of effectiveness in order to be assured that our (lives) are legitimated.'[70]

In a way, this is exactly what the Reformation was about...God has liberated us from the need to make things right...to become self-made Christian success stories...to prove we are worthy...the gift has already been given...now it is a matter of living out of that gift...day after day after day. The quest for anything else anything else ends in our own attempts to secure spiritual security for ourselves. If we are able to attain financial security, health security, material security, technological security...why not spiritual security? In his recent book, the theologian David Congdon reminds us that spiritual security and the salvation that Jesus brings is not 'salvation from suffering or salvation from oppression or salvation from the final judgment or salvation from eternal torment or salvation from

---

[69] Ralph Waldo Emerson, in *Freedom for Ministry*, 103.

[70] Ralph Waldo Emerson, in *Freedom for Ministry*, 104.

our own mortality.' What Jesus liberates us and transforms us for is 'salvation from ourselves,' and not just the 'old sinful self' of classic religious misbehavior, but 'from the illusion that we belong to ourselves.' Jesus saves us 'from our anxious attempts to secure ourselves, from the desire to possess our identity and thus our future, from the struggle to assert our freedom and authority.' Jesus, Congdon believes, saves us from the dangerous belief that we can construct a completely secure world around ourselves.[71]

This freedom from having to assert ourselves and our authority in the world is on full display in our scripture lesson from Matthew in Jesus back and forth with the Pharisees. Why doesn't he ever try to win the arguments and show them who is boss? Why doesn't he feel the need to justify himself or prove himself? What do we do when our authority is called into question? We dig in...we assert ourselves...we pull out our credentials...we prove to everyone how legit we are. Jesus' authority is immediately called into question, and he just stands there and takes it. It does not seem to affect him or move him or cause him to get busy defending himself. Jesus' unique form of authority, does not come, Robert Capon reminds us, by 'what he can prove himself to be,' but on who he is---'he is not in the business of giving arguments that will prove' he has some divine pedigree and right to do what he does, 'he does not reach out to convince us, he simply stands' before us 'in all the attracting/repelling fullness of his (authority) and dares us to believe.'[72] He offers us no crutches, no special proofs, and no fierce arguments, just himself and his ministry and the company he keeps....sinners, tax collectors, and prostitutes.

---

[71] David Congdon, *The God Who Saves*, 80.

[72] Robert Farrar Capon, *Kingdom, Grace, Judgment: Paradox, Outrage, and Vindication in the Parables of Jesus*, 443.

And to Jesus, that is what a 'successful' Christian community looks like. A community that must learn over and over again how impossible it is to think we can be self-made people while being dependent upon God. The Pharisees are not bad people they just want to establish their security on anything besides having to believe and trust Jesus may be the only way to it. Surely we can out-argue him or give him the right answer from the Torah or do these righteous things, certainly we must find our security in something tangible, prove-able, reliable, self-justifying, but their freedom and ours, happens as we are made 'wholly insecure in ourselves but wholly secure in God.'[73]

What makes the tax collectors and prostitutes and sinners exemplary is not their behavior or the way they go about their lives…extortion, self-debasement, and dissolute living are not virtues to be extolled. But this rag-tag community of misfits cannot place their faith in their own virtues, integrity, or achievements and they know it. In the presence of this mysterious Rabbi standing before them and showing them what true faith, true justification, and true freedom look like, they are happy to find their identity in Him rather than in themselves. They don't take themselves as seriously as they take Jesus Christ and the God who keeps company with a whole collection of people that leaves us shaking our heads and laughing to ourselves in disbelief. To be a church is more about being a community that shows up for each other, that forgives each other and that loves it each other than it is about proving certain things or adhering to certain principles or worrying ourselves to death about the status of our security. The church, the Christian community, you and me, we are called and empowered to live with a sense of *hilaritas*, a cheerful refusal to allow the anxieties of our lives or troubles of the world have final authority over us, a

---

[73] David Congdon, *The God Who Saves*, 83.

quiet confidence that refuses to take ourselves so seriously but presses onward joyfully and faithfully trusting that the mysterious work of the crucified and risen Lord among us will dispersed throughout our lives and eventually cover everything.

Those sinners, those tax collectors, and those prostitutes can see better than the Pharisees that Christ has come not only to save them from themselves, but to save them for the sake of each other, so that together, like him, they no longer have to prove their worth but receive it from him and offer it to each other. In a world that measures self-worth and success and importance very differently, may Christ continue save us from ourselves so that we may be truly free…free for each other….and free to be the people he has made room for in Himself. In the name of the Father and the Son and the Holy Spirit, Amen.

Easy Jesus
Matthew 5:38-48

In recent weeks we have heard from Matthew's gospel and from the Sermon on the Mount or the Beatitudes which begins in Matthew 5 and extends through Matthew 7. We have not had much in the way of introduction to this significant and thorough teaching by Jesus so before we engage today's scripture lesson it might be helpful to put this section of scripture in context. Jesus' disciples, as well as all who gathered on the mountainside to take in Jesus' teaching, as well as the people of Israel in Jesus' time would have been aware of the remarkable dichotomy between Jesus' teaching and instruction on the side of the mountain and Moses' receiving of the law and giving it to Israel in Exodus as they prepared to enter the promised land. Often thought to be a Jew and writing to a largely Jewish/Jewish convert audience, Matthew reminds his audience that Jesus is the new Moses, the giver of the law, the teacher of the law, and the fulfillment of the law. Twice in our scripture passage today, Jesus assumes a familiarity and knowledge of ancient Jewish religious and legal requirements as he begins with these words, 'You have heard it said…but I say to you.' One thing to think about as we attend to this word together is whether Jesus is dismissing the earlier teaching and replacing it with a new teaching or if Jesus is reinterpreting the one law of Israel in a more intense and challenging way. Is this a negation or fulfillment of Torah? Listen for the word of God:

> *'You have heard that it was said, "An eye for an eye and a tooth for a tooth." But I say to you, Do not resist an evildoer. But if anyone strikes you on the right cheek, turn the other also; and if anyone wants to sue you and take your coat, give your cloak as well; and if anyone forces you to go one mile, go also the second mile. Give to everyone who begs from you, and do not refuse anyone who wants to borrow from you.*

> *'You have heard that it was said, "You shall love your neighbor and hate your enemy." But I say to you, Love your enemies and pray for those who persecute you, so that you may be children of your Father in heaven; for he makes his sun rise on the evil and on the good, and sends rain on the righteous and on the unrighteous. For if you love those who love you, what reward do you have? Do not even the tax-collectors do the same? And if you greet only your brothers and sisters, what more are you doing than others? Do not even the Gentiles do the same? Be perfect, therefore, as your heavenly Father is perfect.*

WWJD. My sister lives in Austin, Texas, and proudly boasts a t-shirt that reads 'WWWD,' with a picture of a braided and bearded Willie Nelson in the background asking 'what would Willie do?' While Willie Nelson may not be our moral exemplar, this passage brought to mind the early WWJD craze of the late 1990s and early 2000s. What Would Jesus Do was inscribed on bracelets, t-shirts, bumper stickers, keychains, dashboards, rearview mirrors, and baseball caps. What would Jesus do? I always thought we kind of have an out with the saying 'what would Jesus do' because Jesus was the Messiah, the Lord of heaven and earth, and the Savior of the world, who redeemed humanity on a cross and whose life, death, and resurrection inaugurated God's kingdom on earth. That might be 'what' Jesus would do, but I certainly cannot be expected to do that. So that was kind of my out…Jesus would never ask us to do what he would do…but here, we are in deep in the middle of it 38 verses into Matthew 5 and it is getting difficult to take. Jesus may not be saying directly 'do what I would do,' but he is not exactly going easy on us or asking less of us either. Jesus has basically told every religious and law abiding Israelite that what they are doing is not enough, that keeping the faith is not about figuring out what is the least amount I can do or be and still meet the criterion. Rather Jesus intensifies and even alters and extends the law reminding us that we are called to do more than try not to murder our brother and our sister, but we are called to be reconciled together when we have wronged them and when they have wronged us. To be a Christian community Jesus tells us directly is not about figuring out what we need to do or what we can get by with and still get through; it is about becoming something more, salt and light and leaven that flavors the world and reflects the radical love, forgiveness, and community of Jesus Christ. A community that lets go of grudges, a community that practices forgiveness, a community that seeks to measure itself and push itself by a higher standard. One of our favorite family folktales that we still half joke about and half follow is rooted in a story I believe to be true about my grandfather. His children would bring home exemplary grades and knock it out of the park in school and the response was always the same. Rather than a pat on the back, a reward, a victory celebration, what they got was one word: 'excelsior!' You may recognize the word from the Christmas carol 'Angels We have Heard on High' with the refrain, Gloria in Excelsis Deo' Glory to God in the Highest. Well the report card congratulatory response of 'excelsior' was a reminder not to stop or quit or be satisfied but to strive 'ever upward' and 'still higher.' This is what Jesus is doing with the law and responsibilities of Christian community.

Today Jesus presents us with the common legal foundation not just of ancient Israel but all of the ancient near East, the foundation of Hammurabi's code in Babylon: 'an eye for an eye and a tooth for a tooth.' Today this may strike us as retributive and vengeful, but it was actually a legal restraint to prohibit people from overreacting when a crime was committed against them. If someone hit you and knocked out one tooth, then the law limited your response and restrained you from knocking out all of your perpetrator's teeth. But even an eye for an eye and tooth for a tooth is not enough,

Jesus proclaims to his hearers, you are called to resist the evildoer by turning your cheek and responding to those who sue you by giving them the coat of your back and going the extra mile. Jesus is reinterpreting and radicalizing the law to such an extent that all who heard this (and I am including all of us in the equation) had to be both demoralized by just how much Jesus asks from us and perhaps also a bit frustrated with Jesus and what he thinks he can ask of a community of his followers. Easy Jesus was meant to be an ironic analysis of this text, but I think if we added a comma after easy we might get at the sentiments of the crowds on the hillside and our own feelings about Jesus' interpretation of what it means to be the Christian community. Easy, Jesus. Don't you know it is not cool to be a Christian any more…don't you know nobody is going to judge us any more if we drink our coffee and read our paper on Sunday morning. You should just be glad we are here and not working in the yard or sleeping in or catching up on our Netflix binge watching. Easy, Jesus. Before you try to undo all of us and show us that we are all reprobates and wrongdoers of varying stripes and degrees, could you at least acknowledge us and affirm us? Could you at least give us credit for some of our accomplishments and make us feel a little bit comfortable?

Which leads me to my go-to interpretation of this text. My instinctual theological move is to read these very hard teachings about returning no one evil for evil and turning the other cheek, teachings about loving my enemies and praying for them, my go-to move is to then say: the point of easy Jesus saying all this is to show how impossible it is for any of us 'to live up to God's standard of righteousness, and thus all our consciences should be equally convicted that we are sinners in need of grace.'[74] I still

---

[74] Richard Hays, *The Moral Vision of the New Testament*, 320.

In the Meantime

believe that is part of what Jesus is getting at here, but if that is all he was trying to say, he sure does go into a lot of detail and specification about what the Christian community should live like and look like beyond just a people in need of God's grace. None other than the biblical scholar Richard Hays also rejects my interpretation of the text reminding us that these purist teachings of the Sermon on the Mount are not just there to help us recognize all the ways we fall short and to compel us of our need of God's grace, but that Jesus means for these words to be put into practice and be reflected in the way of life and the ways the Christian community lives together.[75] The community Jesus is bringing into being will embody the character of a community in which 'anger is overcome through reconciliation,' desires, lusts, and greed will be restrained, marriage and all our relationships will be honored through lifelong fidelity, we will speak the truth in love, retaliation will be renounced, and love of enemies replaces indifference and hate.[76] This is the community Jesus inaugurated and is bringing into being. No we may not always reflect or feel like it or believe it is something humanly possible. But Jesus does not back away or lower the bar or say you know what, 'less is more.' Wherever we are and wherever we stand in the midst of this challenging teaching, Jesus addresses us as a member within a community that he says lives and loves and forgives in this way. Jesus has already said this is who we are.

So, excelsior. Always upward. Ever higher. Amen.

---

[75] Richard Hays, *The Moral Vision of the New Testament*, 324.
[76] Richard Hays, *The Moral Vision of the New Testament*, 321.

Unlocked
John 20:19-31

¹⁹*When it was evening on that day, the first day of the week, and the doors of the house where the disciples had met were locked for fear of the Jews, Jesus came and stood among them and said, "Peace be with you." ²⁰After he said this, he showed them his hands and his side. Then the disciples rejoiced when they saw the Lord. ²¹Jesus said to them again, "Peace be with you. As the Father has sent me, so I send you." ²²When he had said this, he breathed on them and said to them, "Receive the Holy Spirit. ²³If you forgive the sins of any, they are forgiven them; if you retain the sins of any, they are retained." ²⁴But Thomas (who was called the Twin), one of the twelve, was not with them when Jesus came. ²⁵So the other disciples told him, "We have seen the Lord." But he said to them, "Unless I see the mark of the nails in his hands, and put my finger in the mark of the nails and my hand in his side, I will not believe." ²⁶A week later his disciples were again in the house, and Thomas was with them. Although the doors were shut, Jesus came and stood among them and said, "Peace be with you." ²⁷Then he said to Thomas, "Put your finger here and see my hands. Reach out your hand and put it in my side. Do not doubt but believe." ²⁸Thomas answered him, "My Lord and my God!" ²⁹Jesus said to him, "Have you believed because you have seen me? Blessed are those who have not seen and yet have come to believe." ³⁰Now Jesus did many other signs in the presence of his disciples, which are not written in this book. ³¹But these are written so that you may come to believe that Jesus is the Messiah, the Son of God, and that through believing you may have life in his name.*

In the Meantime

One of the favorite television commercials in our household is a Progressive Insurance Commercial that takes place in a support group of early middle age people coming to terms with the fact that they are becoming their parents...maybe you have seen it. It begins inside an auditorium in support group fashion with a circle of chairs and a group of people sharing their common struggles. As they gather, they share their stories of metamorphosis into their parents Here are a few: 'I text in full sentences...I refer to every child as chief...' another member of the group, wearing knee-high brown socks with sandals confesses to telling every stranger he sees that 'defense wins championships' and the scene closes with a member of the group looking at the open door in the corner and asking who left the door open and if 'we are trying to air condition the world here.'

I thought about this commercial recently on a recent trip to the bookstore when I realized that my idea of a good time has become taking the kids to the bookstore or the library. When did I turn into my parents? I guess it just happens. Well it is on these trips to the bookstore, in spite of trying to enjoy myself and look for a mystery or a thriller or a nice history book, I cannot help but look at what is on offer and really 'hot' in the religion section. And every trip, it is always a disappointment. For starters, the goal of nearly every book in the religion section is no different than any other professional trying to tap into our consumer urges and manufactured needs...promising us instant gratification whether it is our 'best life now,' or our best 'spiritual practices' or how to become spiritually content and happy in life. I remember watching a documentary awhile back about the restaurant industry and saw that apparently seeing the color red makes us hungry and engages our appetite, which is why most restaurants, especially if they have neon lights, have red there somewhere. Red makes us hungry...interestingly, in that same piece, it noted that yellow and brown do not make us hungry or prone to want to sit somewhere and enjoy a meal which if you recall were the two colors of every McDonald's dining area. Get-em in and get-em out, but don't make them enjoy the environment too much...we want the next customers moving through.

Religion sections of the bookstore have those flashing red neon lights, but they are trying to sell titles like 'fulfillment,' 'zen,' 'serenity,' 'success,' 'effectiveness,' 'relevance,' 'becoming the best you,' and none of these states are unworthy pursuits, but none of them really have to do with God. They are all about us. To paraphrase Eugene Peterson, asking the question how can I worship better, how can I experience faith better, how can I be a better Christian, how can I be more effective in 'my' ministry, at the end of the day, these are all very selfish or at least self-centered questions. I remember early on in ministry, not long after leaving seminary, a friend asked me how 'my ministry' was going and I could only respond by saying, 'my ministry' is on life support, but thankfully Jesus is more than holding up his end of things. So I guess you are right, theology ruins everything. I cannot even stand there in the bookstore and enjoy myself but can only stand there and wonder how many years and generations of this type of 'religious self-help' has been unfolding with little to show for itself other than a need to buy the next book that will address the next set of problems or put us back on the road to contentment if this book didn't quite get us there.

And maybe that is the takeaway right there...nothing works...no number of books on acquiring contentment or eradicating our problems or brings us complete tranquility or solving life or becoming a religious success…. none of it works. This past week I was watching a documentary marking the fiftieth anniversary of Martin Luther King, Jr.'s death, and the piece I happened to be watching was filmed from the Riverside Church in New York City where King gave a speech on April 4, 1967, in opposition to the Vietnam War, one year before his assassination. Many of King's colleagues in ministry and in civil rights either disagreed with him on the war or disagreed with him opposing the war publicly, after all, he would be opposing and undermining the very same Johnson administration that had supported King's efforts to pass civil rights legislation. Now he was biting the hand that had so recently helped him. His advisors thought it was a strategic mistake for that exact reason…they needed the administration's support for their civil rights initiatives and to protect and ensure equality in America and here was King risking all that by voicing his opposition to the Vietnam war. I recount all this to remind you that in the life of faith and discipleship, sometimes a conviction of faith and moral conscience does not bring us contentment and fulfillment at all but is a dark night of the soul that makes enemies out of our allies and leads to misunderstanding and frustration.

I also recount all this to remind you how little the mission and purpose of scripture has to do with a me-centered spirituality or religious self-help. Our lesson begins not with a bunch of religious success stories but begins inside a locked-up house with the doors bolted shut and a bunch of fearful, scared, and fainthearted disciples just hoping they could escape their problems and escape all the strange events that had just transpired in Jerusalem. They are not thinking about finding fulfillment, they are thinking about survival. Even though the house is fortified and locked up to keep all the trouble out, the risen Christ appears in their midst with ease, showing his hands and his side and bringing them peace. Whenever the risen Jesus shows up, he brings peace and those in his presence go from fear or trouble or anxiety to rejoicing. In John's words, 'the disciples rejoiced when they saw the Lord.'

And so it goes with us in the life of this Christian community. We are not selling religious self-help or promising to solve everyone's problems. What I do believe we are about here is trying to follow the pattern depicted in our scripture lesson. In spite of our troubles, our problems, our worries, our fragility, our flaws, our broken ways, our locked hearts, our locked souls, our locked minds, Jesus shows up and in the midst of the mess and the troubles and the fears, offers us his peace. And it leads to rejoicing. Christ's presence makes us joyful. It does not necessarily get rid of all the other stuff, it just makes it bearable, it puts it in proper perspective, it marginalizes it, and adds a dimension to our lives that enriches everything else. But even that is not the end of the story. Jesus brings peace and joy, lifting our burdens and unlocking our lives, but things don't end there. In verse twenty-one, Jesus brings peace but then in the same breath says to us that 'as the Father has sent me, so I send you.' Jesus does not walk through our walls and locked doors to grant all our wishes and desires like a genie in a bottle or the religion section at Barnes and Noble but unlocks our lives so that we may be sent into the world to live as his disciples, offering others the life we have in him, and trying our best to reflect his grace and glory in the life of the world.

As the Father sends me, so I send you. That is an extraordinary commission and responsibility. Think about what Jesus does not say…. he doesn't say the Father sent me to tell you how special you are and leave you to wallow in your contentment. He does not say, the Father sent me to fix everything you don't like and to solve all your problems. He does not say, the Father sent me to help you adjust to the challenges and complications of life in the modern world. He says, as the Father has sent me, so I send you. We become our true selves, not by staying where we are or as we are, not in our quest for religious fulfillment, but as we are sent, sent into the world to serve the crucified and risen Lord. And what is extraordinary about that commission is that Jesus compares it to his own incarnation and coming into this world. Jesus says that just as God has sent me to you, so I send you to be the voice of Jesus Christ to those who need encouragement, so I send you to be the hands of Jesus Christ to those who need love and support, so I send you to be the feet of Jesus Christ to those on the edges of the paths we walk.

Friends this may not be what we through we were getting into…this may not be our idea of religious enlightenment…this may not be what we believe we are capable of…but this is who Jesus Christ already said we are…this is who Jesus Christ has already unlocked us to be. We are free to remain prisoners of ourselves…chasing religious fulfillment, focused on ourselves and massaging our own needs…or we can become prisoners of Jesus Christ…and as such, truly free. Amen.

Non-Ending
Mark 16:1-8

When the Sabbath was over, Mary Magdalene, and Mary the mother of James, and Salome bought spices, so that they might go and anoint him. And very early on the first day of the week, when the sun had risen, they went to the tomb. They had been saying to one another, "Who will roll away the stone for us from the entrance to the tomb?" When they looked up, they saw that the stone, which was very large, had already been rolled back. As they entered the tomb, they saw a young man, dressed in a white robe, sitting on the right side; and they were alarmed. But he said to them, "Do not be alarmed; you are looking for Jesus of Nazareth, who was crucified. He has been raised; he is not here. Look, there is the place they laid him. But go, tell his disciples and Peter that he is going ahead of you to Galilee; there you will see him, just as he told you." So they went out and fled from the tomb, for terror and amazement had seized them; and they said nothing to anyone, for they were afraid.

'Terror and amazement seized them...they said nothing to anyone, for they were afraid.' End of story. Or is it?

It is ironic that at the beginning of the story of Jesus Christ, recounted just a few short months ago at Christmas Eve, we began with the words 'fear not'--spoken to Mary and to shepherds out in the feeds watching their flocks by night. 'Fear not,'--we hear upon the arrival of the baby in the manger. But here at the end of Mark's gospel, the end of the narrative concludes with these words: 'and they said nothing to anyone, for they were afraid.' So much for 'fear not.'

It is not surprising that not everyone has been happy with the end of Mark's gospel. In fact, if you read on, Mark's gospel continues past verse eight with two different endings. There is the shorter ending with a brief addendum from Jesus to Peter and then there is a longer ending, verses 9-20, with appearances to Mary Magdalene, the disciples, a commissioning, and then Jesus' ascension. So rather than trying everything up with a nice pastel colored Easter bow, Mark's gospel ends with a big multi-car pile-up, with not one, not two, but three separate endings and Easter arriving not as a tying-all-the-loose-ends together-happy-ending, but as hot mess, with a small gathering of faithful women, the only ones dedicated enough to visit Jesus' tomb, and a cliffhanger of fear and amazement and uncertainty about what is next.

Many of the earliest accounts of Mark's gospel end at verse eight and most biblical scholars largely agree that is there that Mark ended his gospel and that later generations of Christians in Mark's community and beyond, uncomfortable with or wanting a more conclusive ending, added these additional verses and sought to bring some closure to the story and give us the conclusion and decisive ending we so often crave. In a piece written for the *Christian Century* several years ago, entitled, 'Dangling Gospel,' Tom Long shares the story from Donald Juel's commentary on the Gospel of Mark about one of his students who memorized the whole of Mark in order to do a 'dramatic, Broadway-style (one act) reading before a live audience. After careful study, the student had decided to go with scholarly consensus' and end with verse, but at his first performance, when he spoke the last verse, 'he stood there awkwardly, shifting from one foot to the other, the audience waiting for more, waiting for closure, waiting for a proper ending. Finally, after several anxious seconds, he said, 'Amen!' and made his exit. The relieved audience applauded loudly and appreciatively. Upon reflection, though, the student realized that by providing the audience a satisfying conclusion, his 'Amen!' had actually betrayed the dramatic intention of the text. So, at the next performance, when he reached the final verse, he simply paused for a half beat and left the stage in silence. The discomfort and uncertainty within the audience were obvious. And as people exited, the buzz of conversation was dominated by the experience of the non-ending.'[77]

Why stop mid-sentence and mid-action with this small band of women fleeing what they have seen with fear and amazement? My grandfather was a Presbyterian minister in the Dallas and Houston areas for most of his ministry. Very early in the post-World War II period, he also started new churches, one in Fort Worth. My grandfather was not known for mincing words and his persona exerted a kind of powerful prophetic authority that I often wish I had. He was not afraid of uncomfortable conversations or telling you what he thought needed to be done. In one of those early congregations, there was a father who would get his kids ready for church, drive them to Sunday School, drop them off, and then head back home and do the lawn and yardwork and then pick-up the kids at an appropriate time. One day, after watching this routine transpire, my grandfather got in his car, followed the man home and as he was cranking up the lawnmower asked him pointblank when he was going to stop dropping his children off at church and start bringing his children with him to church…the next Sunday, the father was there with his children and would later become in an elder in that church and then later serve as an elder in other churches throughout his life. As you might imagine, his preaching style also had a very direct and confrontational style too

---

[77] Thomas G. Long, 'Dangling Gospel (Mark 16:1-8),' *Christian Century*, 123: 7, (April 4, 2006): 19, and Bob Dunham, *Journal for Preachers*, vol.41, 3 (Easter 2018), 23-26.

and he had a way of often ending sermons with a question that was also an exhortation; 'and now, what are you going to do about it?'

I say all this as a way of wondering if Mark is not ending his discussion of Jesus' resurrection in a similar way. His was the earliest Christian gospel written at a time in which the future of Christianity was very much in doubt. Many of his contemporaries, including Paul and Peter had suffered and lost their lives in great waves of government persecutions. The existence of the Christian community was not a given and there were many followers who under duress or threat of persecution were ready to relinquish the claims of this story. One might even argue that Mark is writing directly to them wondering if they are content to let the story of Jesus' miraculous life, death, and resurrection end because they were afraid to say anything to anyone, captive to their own fear and amazement and secrecy. 'What are you going to do about it?' Mark is asking that early fledgling Christian community. Mark ends verse eight as a hanging exhortation. Hey early Christians, are you going to let the story end here in fear and silence, or are you going to do something about it?

But there is another explanation though. And that is that the story is not intended to have a conclusion at all. Perhaps the story stops at verse eight because Easter is not a nice and happy ending to a spectacular story, but is not an ending at all, but an explosive and miraculous beginning to something that leaves us in fear and amazement. We know the story was not dependent upon the successes or the failures of those early disciples to preserve the Christian story. That is why NT scholar Donald Juel suggests that the ending of Mark is not and ending at all, but a beginning, an overcoming and invasion of the 'power of God that cannot be domesticated or buried or fled or contained.'[78] Two women fleeing a tomb and seized by fear and amazement would not register or make headlines then or now except for the fact that this intrusive and persistent Savior continues to show up in their lives and to direct them to larger purposes than they had ever planned for themselves. Easter was not the conclusion of their lives or their story, but an invasion of God's power into their lives that coopted them for a larger story and purpose than they could have imagined or charted or believed was possible on their quiet journey to the tomb. Easter does not bring closure…it overtakes them…the risen Christ calls them onward and refuses to leave them alone. It is the beginning of a life full of disruptions by God. Jesus keeps showing up in their lives and giving them a vision of a life together as his body that miraculously propels them out of their paralysis of fear and attempts at private isolation.

I rarely watch the academy awards, but last year, for some reason, I watched and did not even turn it off prematurely when at first LaLa Land was awarded best picture only to have it revoked and then correctly awarded to Moonlight. I remember taking some pleasure in watching all these professionals, actors, actresses, motion picture icons, standing around with blank looks on their faces, not knowing what to do or how to fix what just happened. This was not supposed to be happening…they were not trained for this…this was unscripted. Christ's resurrection has a similar effect on his community of followers. It has a similar effect on us. There is no closure, instead we are left with this badgering Savior on the loose in our lives, refusing to stay in the tomb where he belongs and allowing us to have our lives on our own terms. Instead Mark's haunting question finds us too, asking us 'what are you going to do about it'?

---

[78] Bob Dunham, *Journal for Preachers*, vol. 41, 3 (Easter 2018), 24.

In the Meantime

Easter is not the end of the story...the Christ refuses to remain locked up or constrained by death or kept at a respectable distance...and he refuses to leave women and men like us paralyzed in fear and amazement...uncertain of what is next. Christ has died, Christ has risen, Christ will come again. He is the One who comes, the One who is risen from the dead, the One who does not seem to like closure. He does not let us off the hook either, until our lives are part of his story and his mission, and his kingdom, and each one of us, together, become much more than we could have ever made of ourselves on our own.

Christ is risen; not as a miraculous feat or as a special capstone to the end of the story. Christ is risen so that the story does not end...until his kingdom comes. Amen.

www.ingramcontent.com/pod-product-compliance
Lightning Source LLC
Chambersburg PA
CBHW070108120526
44588CB00032B/1390